A Complicated Love Story

A Complicated Love Story

Focus on the Fourth Gospel

V. GEORGE SHILLINGTON

CASCADE *Books* • Eugene, Oregon

A COMPLICATED LOVE STORY
Focus on the Fourth Gospel

Copyright © 2019 V. George Shillington. All rights reserved. Except for brief quotations in critical publications or reviews, no part of this book may be reproduced in any manner without prior written permission from the publisher. Write: Permissions, Wipf and Stock Publishers, 199 W. 8th Ave., Suite 3, Eugene, OR 97401.

New Revised Standard Version Bible, copyright 1989, Division of Christian Education of the National Council of the Churches of Christ in the United States of America. Used by permission. All rights reserved.

Cascade Books
An Imprint of Wipf and Stock Publishers
199 W. 8th Ave., Suite 3
Eugene, OR 97401

www.wipfandstock.com

PAPERBACK ISBN: 978-1-5326-8959-8
HARDCOVER ISBN: 978-1-5326-8960-4
EBOOK ISBN: 978-1-5326-8961-1

Cataloguing-in-Publication data:

Name: Shillington, V. George.

Title: A complicated love story: focus on the fourth gospel. / V. George Shillington.

Description: Eugene, OR: Cascade Books, 2019. | Includes bibliographical references.

Identifiers: ISBN 978-1-5326-8959-8 (paperback) | ISBN 978-1-5326-8960-4 (hardcover) | ISBN 978-1-5326-8961-1 (ebook)

Subjects: LCSH: Bible. John—Criticism, interpretation, etc. | Love—Biblical teaching.

Classification: BS2615.6.L6 S55 2019 (paperback) | BS2615.6.L6 (ebook)

Manufactured in the U.S.A.   10/10/19

In Memoriam

Ruth Wiebe

Contents

Preface | ix

1. Introduction | 1
2. Ambiguous World | 8
3. Key Witness: John the Baptizer | 20
4. Anonymous Mother—Nominal Father | 27
5. Two Inquisitive Neighbors: Different as Night and Day | 37
6. The Brothers | 48
7. Signs of a Super Physician | 58
8. Lazarus of Bethany | 67
9. Concerning "the Jews" | 76
10. Jesus' Inauspicious Entrance into Jerusalem for Passover | 84
11. The Beloved Disciple in the Spotlight | 91
12. Pontius Pilate and the Question of Truth | 115
13. Playing Politics: The Case Against Jesus | 125
14. Temporary Tomb | 135
15. The Reality of Jesus Resurrected | 141
16. Conclusion | 147

Bibliography | 157

Preface

THE URGE TO GENERATE a monograph on the Fourth Gospel of the New Testament, otherwise called "The Gospel of John," has occupied my mind for some time. I think the hesitation to write something substantial through the years came from teaching a course on this book of the New Testament. I discovered that new insights came to the fore in each session of teaching. Students would ask questions I hadn't encountered previously. Year by year went by without anything more from me than a few short articles in journals and sermons in pulpits. In autumn 2017 I taught a noncredit course at Canadian Mennonite University on this Gospel. The course was geared for people interested in sorting through the multifaceted text of the Fourth Gospel. More than thirty people signed up. The discussion was lively, and the questions and comments encouraging. At the close of the last session a woman who sat in the middle of the front row of seats stood and said, "It's complicated." The woman was Ruth Wiebe, who has since passed away. I have dedicated this offering in memory of Ruth.

Ruth's brief comment kept coming back to me. At first I thought it was a criticism of my teaching method. I got over that, and realized the "complication" was present already in the text material we were trying to decipher. Along the way I discovered a tendency among some well-intentioned readers of biblical texts: the parts that are hard to understand should be set aside to allow the familiar parts to occupy our minds. I have come to the conclusion that such a method shortchanges the reader, and implicitly distorts the full weight of the material in the biblical text. It is better to read the text on its terms, however jolting it may be at points, with due respect for its time-and-circumstance in history and culture. That is what I have tried to do in this book. I have sought to write in a way that interested readers will find amenable. Academic specialists in New Testament are definitely included among the prospected readers. I think there are insights and discoveries in

Preface

the chapters that follow that will benefit scholars, even if they disagree with some of my conclusions.

I would be remiss if I did not acknowledge my indebtedness to my principal mentor in the doctoral program at McMaster University, Professor E. P. Sanders. In the academic year 1978–1979 Professor Sanders offered a full-year course on the Fourth Gospel. He started out by asking our group to read the Fourth Gospel, and come to next class prepared to answer some basic questions. One of them was to identify the major theme of this particular gospel. Each of us hesitated. There are so many themes running hither and thither in this Fourth Gospel. It is difficult to settle for one that outshines the others. Eventually we discovered, with some nudging from our patient mentor, that the dominant theme in the Fourth Gospel is love. If we had read the stellar work of C. H. Dodd (*The Interpretation of the Fourth Gospel*) in advance of that session we would have fared rather well. Dodd highlights the acceleration of the theme of love from what he wisely called the Book of Signs to the Book of the Passion.[1]

But as the years have come and gone since that course at McMaster University, I have found that the theme of love is not altogether easy to fathom in the Fourth Gospel. How far and to whom does love (*agape*) extend? Are enemies included in the framework of the Fourth Gospel? And why is one disciple in particular defined and identified as "the disciple that Jesus loved"? No other name is given for this disciple beyond this label. How would the other disciples feel about the special love that Jesus extended to this special disciple? All of this to illustrate how this book got its main title, *A Complicated Love Story*.

I hereby offer a word of thanks to all those who encouraged me to put together the sixteen chapters that follow. Good friend Eckhart listened to my musing over long coffee times. He agreed to read a chapter during the process of writing to test the amiability of the language I was using. He encouraged me to finish the job. Along with him was another friend for coffee time, Harold, who has some quarrel with the tenor and texture of the Fourth Gospel, but still listened to my musings. His preference for "the Synoptic Jesus" came through clearly. This kind of interaction on a personal level was invaluable, and I am grateful for such friends.

My wife Grace is well named. Her patience and kindness toward me is astounding. I enter my study and close the door for hours at a time, and she never complains. I cannot fully repay her generosity and understanding.

---

1. Dodd, *Interpretation of the Fourth Gospel*, 398–99; Lewis, *Four Loves*, 141–70.

Preface

Finally, in an adult class in my home church the leaders asked that I present something challenging and interesting for two sessions, one hour each. I responded by asking permission to offer a reading of two chapters from the book for discussion. I completed that assignment more convinced than ever that the material herein should generate ongoing dialogue and perhaps new ways of interacting with the Fourth Gospel. I trust the content will inspire and encourage every reader to engage the material seriously and sympathetically, and thereby discover love unbounded.

1

Introduction

Charting the Way Ahead

THIS BOOK IS FOR everyone interested in rediscovering the heart and soul of the Fourth Gospel of the New Testament. By "rediscovering" I mean finding meaning and purpose in the various literary episodes and themes that may have eluded the reader to this point, as they did me. Fascinated with this Gospel since my youth, I have taught a course at university for many years on its literary and theological character and nuances. In the process of writing this book I discovered new horizons of understanding not noticed during those years of teaching. The work on such literature is never really complete. It is like an unfinished symphony. I trust this offering will prove fruitful for everyone ready to garner fresh insights from engaging this unique Fourth Gospel.

My main purpose in writing this book is to engage familiar texts and themes again in this beloved Gospel, with a view to enhancing understanding. I would like to know, for example, why the author found it expedient to write this Gospel as he did, in sharp distinction from the other three Gospels, called "Synoptic": seeing with singular vision. Like all fresh approaches to ancient literary texts, especially those of the Bible, this one will exhibit some critical wrestling with the shape and substance of the various texts. The process will involve challenging some traditional interpretations of the early and later Christian communities. I think the effort is just. If it were not so, I would be wasting time, my own and the reader's. I consider the Fourth Gospel to be a complex work of literature in its time, but not a work of fiction. To be sure, there are parts that stretch human imagination almost to breaking point. The author's theological and cosmological imagination comes to expression in many and varied ways in keeping with his time and place in history. What he presents as real historical events are often set forth to make a point that will spur his early-second-century community to greater heights. What follows is a bird's-eye view of what to expect in the ensuing fourteen chapters.

CHURCH LEADERS OF THE THIRD CENTURY ASCRIBED NAMES TO GOSPELS

Let me be abundantly clear here, the author of the Fourth Gospel is anonymous, unlike Paul in his letters to churches he founded. But the particular community of Christ-followers who received the Fourth Gospel would know who he is. (There may be more than one hand behind the extant text. I will use the singular for the sake of tradition.) He was their mentor, and probably the founder of their community. They will recognize his themes and typical vocabulary, and will expect to find some new insights woven into the familiar literary fabric. It is much harder for us in our time and culture to grasp the insights within our postmodern environment today.

The church hierarchy, which came to the forefront a century after the composition of this Fourth Gospel, chose a name for the author. That name thereafter became the name assigned to the Gospel. The name that ancient clerics chose as author of the Fourth Gospel was simply "John." The framers identified him as the son of Zebedee, a Galilean fisherman who became a disciple of Jesus. Moreover, the same ecclesiastical elite concluded that the nameless disciple appearing only in the second main part of the Fourth Gospel, identified as the one whom Jesus loved, was the same "John" who wrote this distinctive Gospel in proper Greek language. Their decision has reigned supreme in church circles to the present time, as though it were chosen by divine inspiration. It wasn't. The anonymity is one of the motifs of this Gospel, and should be respected for what it is. So when I cite a text from the Fourth Gospel in the chapters that follow, I will do so with only the number of the chapter and verse, e.g. 3:16, rather than John 3:16. References to other Scriptures will have the adopted title of the document

INTRODUCTION

in question, together with the number of chapter and verse, e.g. Romans 1:1–7; Matthew 5:31.

FROM SCROLL TO CODEX

In chapter 11 I deal in some detail with the change of writing platform from scroll to codex (book). My reason for doing so is to offer some explanation for the application of specific names to worthy scrolls. In a community such as that of the beloved disciple, the keeper of the scrolls would put important scrolls in a container. Each scroll needed identification on the outside to save time and effort rummaging through the scrolls to find the one required. Otherwise one scroll after another would have to be opened to find the right one. So a slip of papyrus was cut, a specific name inscribed on the slip, and then the inscribed slip pasted on the outside of the scroll for identification. The scroll of the Fourth Gospel was eventually deemed worthy of a place in the developing worldwide church, and thus was copied repeatedly with the same name on the outside, and made available to churches around the Mediterranean. "John" was the name chosen for the Fourth Gospel. That figure was believed to be the author, so the title on the slip of the scroll read, "According to John." And that practice has influenced the interpretation of the anonymous Fourth Gospel to this day. For that reason I have chosen to use "Fourth Gospel" when referring to the document, and "Fourth Evangelist" when referring to the anonymous author who composed this complicated love story. That approach honors the deliberate anonymity of the author.

By the fourth century the invention of the codex, or book format, had taken hold. The book could carry within its binding a variety of literary material. Eventually every document of the Bible was incorporated into one codex. The invention accommodated the wider distribution of a collection of documents. Reading from a book by turning pages was much more convenient than unrolling a scroll. The Fourth Gospel was first written on a papyrus scroll. By the end of the fourth century it was canonized, and incorporated into a codex along with other canonized books resulting in the Christian Bible, made up of thirty-nine documents taken over from the Hebrew Bible of Judaism, and twenty-seven documents composed in Greek by leaders in the Christian church. Saint Jerome (347–420 CE) translated most of the two-part Bible into Latin, thereafter known as the Vulgate.

Influenced, no doubt, by the Vulgate, Latin became the sacred language of the church Mass, and remained so for many centuries.

IDENTITY OF THE FAITH COMMUNITY THAT FIRST RECEIVED THE FOURTH GOSPEL

It is not easy to decipher the real identity of a group of readers from the character of writing in one document. That there was a specific group of believers in Jesus Messiah to whom the Fourth Gospel was addressed can be stated with confidence. Altogether there are four documents that exhibit the same linguistic, theological, and conventional pattern: the Fourth Gospel, and the three epistles under the title "John." Love is a significant theme in all four documents. The symbol of light is also prominent in the first epistle, as it is in the Gospel. The estimated time frame of the four documents is ca. 95–110 CE. The Fourth Gospel would be the first of the four documents, insofar as the epistles carry echoes of the theology, language, and concerns of the Gospel.

The common language of the community would have been Greek, not Hebrew or Aramaic. Moreover, the location of the community that received the Fourth Gospel would almost certainly have been located in a Greek-speaking part of the Roman world. The composition of the group at the time of writing the Fourth Gospel may well have been a mixture of Jews and gentiles, although the likelihood of a large number of Jewish believers in Jesus is slim. Echoes of Paul's thought in his missionary letters to his churches come through in the Fourth Gospel especially. The community of the Beloved Disciple may owe its existence to that mission. Paul was Jewish, but accommodated gentiles in the new messianic community of Jesus. By the turn of the second century, however, the new leaders of reconstituted Judaism put pressure on Jewish members in the Christian churches to recant and return to the synagogue. So the composition of the community of the beloved disciple at the beginning of the second century would have been largely gentile.

THE GUIDING THEME OF LOVE ABOVE ALL

I think it is safe to say that love permeates the Fourth Gospel, the second main part in particular. The two principal parts of the Fourth Gospel are rightly called "the Book of Signs" (chapters 2–12), and "the Book of the

INTRODUCTION

Passion" (chapters 13–20). Chapter 21 is an appendix. While the theme of love is clearly evident in the Book of Signs, it is overflowing in the Book of the Passion. The love of Jesus for his disciples is unwavering. On the basis of that unconditional love the disciples are asked to love one another. Love is, in short, the way of God and the way to God. One of the most famous verses in the Fourth Gospel is 3:16. But it is also strangely complex. It is said in that promising text that God loved the world so much that he provided his only Son to bring that love to life in the human family, which Jesus did through his life and ministry, but especially through his death.

Hence, the second main part of the Fourth Gospel has love overflowing through the life and work of Jesus of Nazareth. To complicate matters even more, there is one disciple that Jesus loves above all the others. He comes across in the second part of the Fourth Gospel as a symbolic figure, while operating as a truly human character. He outperforms all the other disciples, including especially Peter. As a symbolic disciple he points the way for other disciples to follow. As a historical figure he is flawless in his character, perfect in his commitment to Jesus, and without blemish in his everyday behavior. The reader will have to decide what to think of this rather enigmatic figure as he comes through in the relevant chapters.

Two further points on the dominant theme of love in the Fourth Gospel must suffice. First, in the appendix of chapter 21 Jesus tests Peter's love for him. The beloved disciple stands aside as witness to the three movements in the test, and also its outcome. Peter fails the test. His love for Jesus is less than it should be. I develop this interesting story in chapter 11. Second, we find a sharp dialogue in chapter 8 between Jesus and "the Jews," presumably meaning "some Jews" from the Pharisees who question the way Jesus operates with his disciples and others. The response of Jesus to the critique from "the Jews" comes across as belittling rather than loving. The statement is severe: "You [Jews] are from your father the devil, and you choose to do your father's desires. He was a murderer from the beginning and does not stand in the truth, because there is no truth in him. When he lies, he speaks according to his own nature, for he is a liar and the father of lies" (8:44).

DECIPHERING THE MOTIF OF ANONYMITY

I consider anonymity a recurring motif in the Fourth Gospel, not an oversight and not an accident. What to make of it is another matter. Atop the list of instances of anonymity is the nameless mother of Jesus. Whereas

Matthew and Luke make much of the mother of Jesus, named Mary, the Fourth Evangelist not so much. The figure of the mother of Jesus is highlighted in two auspicious occasions: at the scene of Jesus's first sign in Cana of Galilee on the occasion of a wedding feast, and at the foot of the cross at the occasion of Jesus's crucifixion. In neither setting is the mother of Jesus named. Otherwise she is effectively out of the picture in the Fourth Gospel. Ironically, Joseph is named as the father of Jesus at two points in the unfolding drama (1:45; 6:42).

The woman at the well (chapter 4) doubtless had a name. We shall never know. But her character and her probing questions and her missionary zeal is manifest. She is purposely portrayed as an honest, yet misguided, inquirer eager to have the living water that Jesus promises. Notably, the woman is a Samaritan who is more appreciative of Jesus and his teaching than many of his own people. She can worship the God of the universe along with every other human being, for "God is spirit, and those who worship [God] must worship in spirit and truth" (4:24). That is, God is neither Jew nor Samaritan, but Creator of both, along with everyone and everything else besides.

The outstanding case of anonymity I have mentioned in passing—let me fill that out further. The nameless disciple that Jesus loved deserves a name, but receives none in the Gospel in which his blameless character is abundantly evident. Interpreting the literary motif of anonymity is both frustrating and fulfilling. To fill in the anonymous blank with a proper name pulled out of the blue accomplishes nothing, except to make us modern readers more comfortable. And I am one of them. For example, I make a case in chapter 11 for another name and identity for the very special follower of Jesus behind the anonymous cover label: "the disciple whom Jesus loved."

ACQUAINTANCE WITH THE SYNOPTIC GOSPELS, OR THE TRADITION BEHIND THEM

I have mentioned briefly already that the Fourth Gospel echoes some of Paul's genuine letters. Those letters were not collected until the latter years of the first century, and became available to communities such as that of the beloved disciple. The major theme of love in the Fourth Gospel probably draws positively on such Pauline texts as 1 Corinthians 13, the great love-chapter of the New Testament. The same cannot be said for the relationship of the Fourth Gospel to the Synoptic Gospels.

The three Synoptic Gospels of Mark, Matthew and Luke, or the traditions on which they rely, predate the composition of the Fourth Gospel. Furthermore, the Fourth Evangelist appears to be aware of them, but challenges parts of the Synoptic story. Loud echoes of key texts from one or another of the Synoptic Gospels come through in the Fourth Gospel. Here is one example: "As they led [Jesus] away, they seized a man, Simon of Cyrene, who was coming from the country, and they laid the cross on him, and made him carry it behind Jesus" (Luke 23:26; Mark 15:21). The Fourth Evangelist will have none of that: "And [Jesus] carrying the cross by himself, he went out to what is called The Place of the Skull" (19:17). Similarly, the opening Prologue to the Fourth Gospel effectively renders the two birth narratives of Matthew and Luke inoperative, especially with respect to bestowing privileged status on Mary (See 1:1–18).

THE MOTIF OF SIGNS POINTING TO TRUTH (OR REALITY)

One of the fascinating features of the Fourth Gospel is the distinction between the first twelve chapters and the last nine chapters. Positive signs of the in-breaking kingdom of God mark the first twelve. The signs are not ultimate Reality, otherwise called Truth, but they point in the direction of its appearance. The last nine chapters are all about the ultimate Reality that Jesus inaugurates by going to his death for the sake of the world and its inhabitants. The repeated saying, "My hour has not yet come," on the lips of Jesus, and also from the narrator, marks the first eleven chapters (2:4; 7:6, 8, 30; 8:20). By chapter 12:22 Jesus announces: "The hour has come for the Son of Man to be glorified" (see also 16:32; 17:1). From that point to the end of the Gospel, the focus is on the self-sacrifice of Jesus on behalf of the world that God loves, despite its shortcomings (3:16–17).

Truth is a major focus in the Fourth Gospel. The idea is that of the undying character of the eternal life that Jesus represents: that which outlasts the ravages of time and mortality. It implies more than "telling the truth," although that aspect is clearly implied. The promise from Jesus to "the Jews who had believed in him" is worth pondering for everyone else as well: "You will know the truth, and the truth will make you free" (8:31–32).

2

Ambiguous World

THE TERM "WORLD" IS more ambiguous and more plentiful in the Fourth Gospel than in any literature I have read to date. From beginning to end the focus returns to that loaded Greek term *cosmos* (world) in an effort to figure out its significance for human life and thought. How did "world" come into being? What exactly constitutes "world" in the Fourth Gospel? Is the human experience of "the world" positive or negative? Or is it a mixture of both?

When I reflect on these questions my mind turns invariably to Robert Frost's long poem, "The Lesson for Today." In that poem Frost proposes an epitaph, later inscribed on his tombstone, whether he intended it to appear there or not: "I had a lover's quarrel with the world." I find that crisp yet cryptic line worthy of reflection, especially so in relation to the abundance of "world" in the Fourth Gospel. The term occurs in that Gospel no fewer than seventy-nine times, compared to twenty-one times in all three Synoptic Gospels combined. I realize frequency of a term does not of itself prove much one way or another. Yet the significant numerical presence of a freighted term in an important document does signal something about the author's interest in the subject. By comparison, one would expect the term "God" (*theos*) to be superabundant in the Fourth Gospel, but "world" outnumbers "God."

David Paul Kirkpatrick, film producer and studio executive, picked up on Robert Frost's epitaph, and reflected on its evocative energy for coming to grips with his own experience of the world as follows: "I wonder if

[Frost's epitaph] isn't the summation of so many of our lives... We fall in love with the world, it becomes our sustenance, our addiction, our endless well of dreams. It disappoints us, it gives us praise, it disgraces us, and makes us victorious, and we look for it, as if a lover, for validation" (see his blog at Davidpaulkirkpatrick.com). So "the world" is the human habitat wherein all thought, language, and action are shaped and executed for good or ill, until "world" calls a permanent halt to our daily round of mental and physical activity in time and place.

Time now to explore the rather complicated story of "the world" that parades across the literary landscape of the Fourth Gospel.

THE *WORD* AND THE *WORLD* IN THE PROLOGUE (1:1–18)

What is usually called "the prologue" to the Fourth Gospel consists of the opening eighteen verses in modern English Bibles. It is written in Hellenistic (Greek) style and thought. Scholars have compared the thought pattern and vocabulary with those of a Jewish scholar named Philo who lived and worked in the city of Alexandria in Egypt. He was a contemporary of Jesus (ca. 20 BCE–ca. 50 CE). Philo had studied philosophy, especially that of Plato, and sought to interpret his Jewish Bible in terms of Greek philosophy. He left behind a significant number of his works for us to probe and ponder. A major theme throughout Philo's books is that of *logos* (word, reason, wisdom, etc.). And one of his striking metaphors is *phōs* (light, insight, etc.). Both of these keywords are prominent also in the prologue to the Fourth Gospel, which sets the stage for the unfolding of the rest of the story.

Inquisitive readers of the opening verse in an English edition will find it as striking as it is puzzling: "In the beginning was the Word, and the Word was with [the] God, and the Word was God." If the human mind could imagine the beginning of time, the Word was there already. Perhaps we should pry open that capitalized "Word" in the first verse. The Greek term is *logos*. That Greek noun implies reason, creative imagination, insight, thought, generative mental energy, etc. We have the term variously enshrined in our English vocabulary: biology, geology, theology, archaeology, and, of course, logic. So the Word was there already at the beginning, face-to-face with "the Divinity/God." Were there two entities before time and matter, or only one? The verse continues: "and the Word was God." That seems to contradict the first part of the verse. If the Word was in a face-to-face relationship with the Divinity/God at the beginning, how could the Word then be God? Greek grammar really does help here. When a Greek article is present with a noun, it signals identity. When there is no article with the noun, as in the last part of verse 1, it implies character. So the character of "the Word" was the same as that of the Divinity/God.

But that is not the end of the puzzlement in the prologue. What follows verse 1 is the English male pronoun, he/him. So we are given to think thereby that "the Word" in the beginning was a male being. It comes so easily to English-speaking Christian readers who have read the whole prologue to think of the historical figure of Jesus as identical with "the Word" in the first verse. After all, they have read at verse 14 that "the Word became flesh" (1:14), and is thereafter identified as the male figure of Jesus Messiah (1:17). Such a thought would be shockingly impossible to Philo. For him, the divine Word (*logos*) could never become a mortal, subject to the temporal world with its inveterate ravages, including pain and death. Furthermore, it behooves Christian readers to ask if "the Word" returned to the original position in relation to the Divinity/God following the death of his mortal flesh.

How does this Prologue relate to the birth narratives that appear variously in Matthew and Luke? It doesn't relate. Unlike those two birth narratives, the Fourth Gospel gives all the honor and glory to Creator God for bringing the Son, Jesus, into the world. The mother of Jesus is totally absent from every sentence in this masterful Prologue. It is sufficient for the Fourth Evangelist to state that the creative Word that was with God "became flesh and lived among us, and we have seen his glory, the glory as of a father's only son, full of grace and truth" (1:14). The ending of the Prologue reveals that the creative Word was embodied in the historical person of Jesus. I think it is fair to say that the Fourth Evangelist was probably aware of the Gospels of Matthew and Luke, and dissociates himself and his Gospel from them. Intuitively he may have felt that the figure of Mary in the birth narratives could become an icon of worship under the title, "Mother of God." I find it hard to think of such an imaginative construction. Whether or not the Fourth Evangelist envisioned such a pattern of thought, it did happen in later church traditions. But according to his carefully stated Prologue he will have nothing to do with such honor going to the woman who bore Jesus. The ending to the Prologue is telling: "Grace and truth came through Jesus Christ. No one has ever seen God. It is God the only son, who is close to *the Father's heart*, who has made him known" (1:17–18). The mother of Jesus is completely out of the picture of the Word coming into the world.

But now we must come to the main point for our purposes: How do the creative Word and the material world relate to each other in the prologue? Here is how the relevant text reads at 1:9-10: "The true light, which enlightens everyone, was coming into the world. He was in the world, and the world came into being through him; yet the world did not know him." Keep in mind that the pronouns "he" and "him" refer back to "the Word" that was present in the very beginning with the Divinity, not yet forward to the historical figure of Jesus. By this account "the world" was good, but people who came to occupy the world did not recognize its origin and character: "the world did not know him" who is the light that "enlightens everyone" in the world. This is where the historical figure of Jesus comes into focus in verses 14–18. The reason for his coming into the habitat for humanity in the first century was to reveal to human minds the true character of the Creator of "the world."

A nagging question still remains, however. Is "the world" a safe and wholesome sphere for human habitation in time and space? The very idea is filled with mystery. The world is more than the geological planet Earth. It is that to be sure. But it is also the air we breathe; the water we drink; the relationships we form and those we refuse; the language we use to communicate; the law courts that purport to deliver justice for all; the holiday we take near an ocean; it is the telescope we use to view other planets; the airplanes we use to fly from one place to another; the crashes that happen; the deals we make and break; the taxes we pay; the investments we evaluate; the clothes we wear; the relationships we form and fracture; the explorations to other planets; the pollution we pour into the atmosphere; the animals we slaughter for food; the tsunamis and earthquakes and tornados; the battles human beings wage against each other. "World" is the sphere of life in which we live in the material universe, the love we share, the adversity we bear, and the death we die. And if there should be life forms on other planets, as seems possible, they are also included in "world."

All of this and so much more is the stuff of "the world" that occupies the mind of the Fourth Evangelist, as it does our own. The various particulars of "world" differ from one time frame to another, but the puzzling story of "the world" is the same from one generation to another. One thing is sure: there is no escaping "the world." We are born into it unwittingly, and we leave it unwillingly. No wonder the Fourth Evangelist probes the subject to the extent that he does, and tries to explain all the while how Creator-God and temporal World correlate, or not.

THE LENGTH TO WHICH GOD GOES TO SAVE THE WORLD (3:16–17)

I would be completely remiss if I left untapped the best known and most loved verse in the Fourth Gospel, if not in the entire Bible. "For God so loved the world that he gave his only son, so that everyone who believes in him may not perish but may have eternal life" (3:16). The next statement reinforces the positive energy of this beloved verse 16: "Indeed, God did not send the Son into the world to condemn the world, but in order that the world might be saved through him" (3:17). The view expressed so lavishly and forcefully in these two sentences leaves no doubt that the divine idea of the world, together with the human experience of it, are worth saving. Of course, the same idea and experience imply strongly that something is not right with "the world." People who live in the world also perish invariably from the world. And that is the inherent problem.

When I was a young man of twenty-two years I took an evening course at a college in Toronto, Canada. The instructor drew attention to 3:16 briefly, but deliberately, to clarify the point about God loving the world. He said "the world" in 3:16 means the world of sinners, not the physical and cultural world in which people live and breathe. So many years later I am still pondering that notion, and am still not convinced that the addition of "sinners" to the text clarifies the story in any meaningful way. It seems to me rather important to pay close attention to the actual terms of the text before we propose additional words and ideas that may or may not correlate with the words on the printed page before our eyes.

"Sinners" in biblical context are lawbreakers; specifically those who disregard and thereby violate the law of God represented in the Hebrew Torah of Israel and Judaism. The message of 3:16–17 deals with the character of the world into which human beings are born and are obliged to live for a while, and then perish from the world. The text affirms the world of time and space in which people live, but the same text also asserts that the beloved world robs human beings of the life they grow to love. So 3:16–17 of the Fourth Gospel holds out a promise that "the world" that we experience daily is not the end of the story of God. There is eternal life, says the text, as compared to the time-sensitive life we all live on planet Earth. And the eternal kind can be had through this special redeemer known as Jesus. He is called Son of God, and as such has the power to ransom those bound to the world through physical birth and cultural mores. The requirement for this newness of life is through believing in the grace and love of Jesus to make the life-giving transfer happen.

Hence the later statement of Jesus in this Gospel to a woman named Martha of Bethany at the death of her brother: "Jesus said to her, 'I am the resurrection and the life. Those who believe in me, even though they die, will live, and everyone who lives and believes in me will never die'" (11:25). The principal problem with "the world" of humankind, in short, is its transience. People are born into "the world" with an urge to live forever because life in "the world" allows us humans to taste the good and wish it would not end. But "forever" does not happen in "the world." The Fourth Gospel holds out to everyone in "the world" the hope of eternal life in relation to Jesus Messiah. This is largely the positive theme throughout the entire Gospel, sharply focused at 3:16–17.

Compare that hope-filled vision with the notorious pessimism of Shakespeare's Macbeth at the death of Lady Macbeth:

> Out, out, brief candle!
> Life's but a walking shadow, a poor player
> That struts and frets his hour upon the stage
> And then is heard no more. It is a tale
> Told by an idiot, full of sound and fury,
> Signifying nothing. (Act 5, Scene 5)

Macbeth is a nihilist here. He considers human life to be meaningless, "signifying nothing." The Fourth Evangelist would object strenuously, it seems to me. Life in time-and-world is a foretaste of life beyond time-and-world. Just as limited life in time-and-world is gift, so is eternal life gift beyond measure and beyond world as we experience it.

Attention to each and every statement about "the world" in the Fourth Gospel would extend this chapter well beyond its proper limit. Other subjects deserve recognition. So we must content ourselves with only one more critical text in which "the world" plays a significant role in the unfolding drama of the Fourth Gospel.

A LONG PRAYER FOR LOVED ONES REMAINING IN THE WORLD (17:1–26)

Chapter 17 carries a long prayer of Jesus in which he appeals to Father-God on behalf of his followers remaining in the world after he is gone. How the author would have gained access to such a personal prayer of this length remains a mystery. It is doubtful that Jesus would have committed such a prayer to writing. There is otherwise no evidence that Jesus wrote anything on durable parchment or papyrus during his lifetime. I hesitate to suggest that the Fourth Evangelist knew enough about the ministry and mind of Jesus to create the substance of the prayer as reflecting the thought and ministry of Jesus.

"World" occurs eighteen times throughout the prayer in chapter 17. The aim of the prayer appears to justify the world on the one hand and point up its shortcomings on the other. The Word of God created the world initially, and positioned humankind within its sphere, including good people of faith epitomized especially in the disciples of Jesus. The prayer is offered up for the protection of the faithful, as they await eternal life not possible in the material world.

I have selected eight images from the prayer to illustrate the motive and vision inherent in it with respect to the disciples left behind in the "world" after the death of Jesus. A few sentences for each one must suffice.

"The hour has come" (17:1)

The Fourth Gospel has two rather distinct parts, which C. H. Dodd called the Book of Signs (2:1—12:26) and the Book of the Passion (12:27—20:31). At the beginning of the Book of Signs, Jesus announces that his hour has not yet come (2:4). That signals that he is still in mission and ministry in the world. When we reach the end of the Book of Signs Jesus announces: "The hour has come for the son of Man to be glorified" (12:23). Mission accomplished. Then at the beginning of the prayer in chapter 17 he confirms the fact: "the hour has come." Time and world go hand in hand in the Fourth Gospel. The "hour" for Jesus is that of transition out of the "world" in which time dominates, into the sphere of eternity in which the ravages of time no longer hold sway. But the hour of transition involves death wherein the aspects of world and time vanish forever. So "the hour" of transition for Jesus is one of victory and glory surpassing the hours of a clock: surpassing "the world," yet not bringing the world to an end.

"The glory that I had in [God's] presence before the world existed" (17:5)

It is a challenge to understand the meaning of such a phrase as this. It stretches the imagination to the limit—mine at least—to conceive of any form of being outside of time and world; any form of self-consciousness without a nervous system. Yet there it stands in this phrase in a prayer of Jesus: the first personal pronoun singular, "I." In some sphere before and beyond time and world, the "I" (*ego*) inherent in the historical figure of Jesus experienced the glory of eternal God. We human beings know the world well enough, with all of its challenges in time and space. We think and speak from within that sphere of knowing. When we look beyond our world of everyday experience we still look for other planets and other suns, and we use our scientific, earthly understanding to do so. And I have noticed that when religious people speak of the eternal sphere they still bring their everyday experience of the world to the table. So here we are bumping up against mystery again in this statement of Jesus at 17:5 in which he speaks of the glory he had in God's presence before the cosmos-world existed.

"Those whom you [Father/God] gave me from the world" (17:6)

The reference implies all those who followed the life and thought of Jesus, not only the twelve disciples exclusively. The number twelve is symbolic of Israel, whereas the unknown number of followers represents "the world" of humankind. What is interesting in this statement in 17:6 is that God is honored for giving the unknown number of followers to Jesus from the world. This is quite different from the refrain, "I have decided to follow Jesus." In the prayer, Creator-God is credited with giving representatives from the world to Jesus. If God gave the "world" to humankind in the first place, why not those "from the world" in the new sphere of eternity that Jesus represents in the second place?

"I am no longer in the world, but they are in the world" (17:11)

Jesus speaks in the Book of the Passion as though he had already departed from the world into the new sphere of existence. Hence the thought that he is already transformed out of flesh and blood, and speaks from that other realm beyond "world." It reads as though the Word that was present at the beginning with God (1:1) has returned to that nontemporal state: no longer in the flesh (1:14). He prays from that supreme vantage point for those still in the "world," as he once was himself. And what is the specific prayer request?

> "I am not asking you [Father/God] to take them out of the world" (17:15)

The request is not that God do for them what he did for Jesus: take them out of the world to be in the eternal presence of God. No. Jesus asks that they be protected from the evil one while they are still residents in the world. They are physical beings still. They need to buy food to remain in the world; they need shelter while they abide there; they need to provide for their family while they live in the world. As long as the followers of Jesus require the life-giving ingredients of the world, it will be difficult for them not to be part of the fabric of the social, political, and economic features of the world. So the prayer is for the protection of the ones who believe in Jesus while they remain in the world. The inference is that "the world" is not a safe place for those who challenge the vain and selfish brokering that goes on in the otherwise life-sustaining world.

> "The world has hated them because they do not belong to the world" (17:16)

This statement simply confirms that the people who belong to the Jesus-way are at odds with the people who use the world for personal ambition. Hence, the hatred against the surviving followers of Jesus persists among those who reject his way of life and thought. People of Jesus operate by a different standard from that of the world: "they do not belong to the world."

> "You have sent me into the world, so I have sent them into the world" (17: 17–18)

The two parts of the sentence correlate. Creator-God sent Jesus into the world to call to account those who spawn human corruption of the good in the world. While he was in the world Jesus called together a faithful and honorable band of people to continue to do for the world what he had done while he was alive in the flesh. The idea of "sending" the faithful followers into the world signals mission. Of course, the risk of mission is reaction from those who like the world the way it is, especially so if the world can be used to accommodate selfish ambition. The way of Jesus, and of those whom he sent into the world, is life-giving, but also costly.

"[You/Father] have loved them even as you have loved me" (17:23)

Not surprisingly, the theme of love surfaces in the prayer. The prayer is, after all, integral to the Book of the Passion of Jesus in which the theme of love abounds. What does it mean to be loved by Creator God? Surely it must mean a lot! But the love of God for good people of the world does not consist in sentimental values, much less in a false promise of a carefree life devoid of pain and death. The love that God bestowed on the Son is the same kind granted to those who belong to the Son. That means that if God spared not the Son, neither will God spare those who belong to the household of faith in Jesus the Son. God loves them as he loved Jesus who went to the cross for the sake of others. It reads like a complicated love story. And sure enough, to minds estranged from God the story lacks appeal. But to people attuned to Jesus Messiah, the love of God is a many splendored thing, mirrored especially in martyrs who offered themselves up in the cause of truth and justice and forgiveness. Martyrs, otherwise known as witnesses, know love divine that transcends romanticized love.

To conclude, the combined theme of the creative "Word" and the created "World" in the Fourth Gospel stretches human imagination to the limit, and not least responsible interpretation of the relevant texts. The "world" is the habitat for humanity initiated by the pre-world power of the Divinity we call "God." The idea of "world," as it comes across abundantly in the Fourth Gospel, is not limited to the substance and atmosphere and life force related specifically to planet Earth. What happens on Earth is strongly focused, to be sure, but "world" (*cosmos*) encompasses the universe of galaxies, solar systems, planets and stars and the controlled space they occupy. "All things came into being through [the divine Word], and without [the Word] not one thing came into being" (1:3).

There may be life forms on some other planets, but the Fourth Evangelist is chiefly concerned with the interaction of human lives with each other as they live together on this small planet, Earth. That environment is "the world" in view for the most part in the Fourth Gospel. And God who created that "world" is said to love it, and especially the human species that lives on it and from it. Human life, like all life in the time-centered world, is subject to suffering and death, and that without exception. The problem for "the world," from my reading of the relevant texts, is when human beings fail to recognize that they do not own any part of "the world" in which they live. They are tenants merely. Yet one after another vies unduly for position and power, often at the expense of others, and thereby debases the creation brought about by the Divinity.

The Word made flesh in the person of Jesus points the way to salvation and wholeness, and not least eternal life. Some people of the world believe in Jesus and follow him, because he holds out eternal life to them, the greatest gift. But not everyone is willing to accept the gift, choosing vainly to build up self-propelled power that perishes at death. Yet God through the incarnate Word loved the world of people so that they would not perish, but attain life eternal. That is a major theme in the Fourth Gospel.

ADDENDUM: EXPEDITION TO A NEW PLANETARY HOME FOR THE HUMAN FAMILY

In a television program on Ireland's RTE 2, April 8, 2018, Stephen Hawking, among others, predicted that the human family would be obliged to migrate to another planet in a hundred years because of reaching the high-water mark of the population of Earth by that time. There seems to be no alternative. The population on Earth in 2018 is 7.5 billion people. At the beginning of the twentieth century, the population on Earth was only one billion.

Setting up a colony for human life on another planet would require some essentials. It would have to be Earth-like, with its own sun amenable to body temperature, and sufficient water supply. The universe is unimaginably enormous, and still expanding. But planets and their stars that would sustain human life are not plentiful and not easily accessible from the vantage point of Earth. One planet said to hold out some promise for human life is Proxima Centauri b, according to the scientists. But according to the present state of spaceship technology it could take an estimated 54 years to reach it. And there is no sure evidence of water on Proxima Centauri b, and none about the temperature. Whatever planet may be found, it is now apparent that planet Earth will not support the current rate of growth in human population indefinitely.

Alternately, the persistent increase in population on Earth in the last century could be politically curtailed at a sustainable level in the future. I have the notion that such an alternative would meet up with significant resistance. All the while, the population problem on Earth could persist to the point of widespread hunger and unsustainable growth in building projects to accommodate families and factories. I trust the next generation of physicists, scientists, politicians, and no less clear-thinking religious people will take seriously the population problem facing planet Earth and its people. "For God so loved the *cosmos*/world that he gave his only son, so that everyone who believes in him may not perish but may have eternal life" (3:16).

3

Key Witness: John the Baptizer

JOHN, SON OF ZACHARIAH the priest (Luke 3:2), bears witness to Jesus in two settings in the early chapters of the Fourth Gospel, 1:19–34 and 3:22–30. Both men were administering water baptism on those who chose to join their respective company of faithful Jewish followers. Jesus is said to have baptized more disciples than John (4:1). But then the narrator immediately adds an aside, "it was not Jesus himself but his disciples who baptized" (4:2). While the effective function of the baptism in each case is not stated boldly, we may assume that it marks a new course of religious thought and action within the context of Palestinian Judaism of the day. In short, the two prophetic figures, John and Jesus, were creating two new subversive communities within the context of Palestinian Judaism, accountable, as it was, to imperialist Rome through the governor, Pontius Pilate.

But the Fourth Evangelist does not support the propagation of two new subsets of radical Judaism. John's group of faithful followers should give way to the community of the kingdom bringer, Jesus of Nazareth. "He [Jesus] must increase, but I [John] must decrease" (3:30). It is likely that a community honoring John the Baptizer still existed when this Fourth Gospel was composed at the end of the first century. There appears to be a respectful urging going on in the early part of the Fourth Gospel for the community of John the Baptizer to abandon its distinctive stance in deference to the community of Jesus Messiah.

Key Witness: John the Baptizer

A TEMPORARY WITNESS TO A PERSON OF GREATER RANK AND MISSION

It is rather well-known from the three Synoptic Gospels that the baptism John administered had to do with repentance, a turning away from compromise and corruption within the religion of current Judaism. That is not the emphasis in the Fourth Gospel. "Repentance"—noun or verb—does not occur even once in this Gospel. John the Baptizer's function, according to the narrator, is to bear witness to the superiority of the one who comes after him, namely Jesus. Here is how the witness of John operates within the context of the greater ministry of Jesus in the context of Jewish leadership and worship.

> This is the testimony given by John when the Jews sent priests and Levites from Jerusalem to ask him, "Who are you?" He confessed and did not deny it, but confessed, "I am not the Messiah." And they asked him, "What then? Are you Elijah?" He said, "I am not." "Are you the prophet?" He answered, "No." Then they said to him, "Who are you? Let us have an answer for those who sent us. What do you say about yourself?" He said,
>
> "I am [a] voice of one crying out in the wilderness,
> 'Make straight the way of the Lord,'"
> as the prophet Isaiah said (1:19–23).

It is clear from this text that John the Baptizer belonged to the Judaism of his time. In particular, the ones who came to investigate his mission hailed from the temple of Jerusalem, the sacred center of Jewish faith. The inquisitors were priests and Levites, concerned about the status and ministry that John was propagating through his baptism of Jewish people. The shape of his threefold answer to the priests and Levites about his identity is striking by the way it diminishes John in deference to Jesus. Observe their questions: 1. "Who are you?" 2. "What then? Are you Elijah?" 3. "Are you the prophet?" The diminishing shape of John's three corresponding replies is telling:

1. "I am not the Messiah."
2. "I am not."
3. "No."

A Complicated Love Story

All three responses are negative. John the Baptizer is not the redeemer of Israel, not the kingdom-bringer, not even the prophet-forerunner to the Messiah. He is witness merely to the long expected anointed One of God. When the Jewish leaders push him to give his own positive identity as a Jewish activist, his reply is totally unassuming: "I am [a] voice." Nothing more. Not *the* voice, as though John's voice carried foreordained authority, as some translations suppose. John's is merely "a voice of one crying out in the wilderness, 'Make straight the way of the Lord'" (1:23). The Lord matters above all else; the vocal witness of the radical Baptizer not so much.

It's fine for John to testify that he is only "a voice" and nothing more. But the priests and Levites, sent by the Pharisees (1:24), are not persuaded, and for good reason. John had become a prominent figure in the Jewish environs of Palestine. This is borne out without apology in the three Synoptic Gospels. In those texts, Jesus declares: "among those born of women no one has arisen greater than John the [Baptizer]" (Matt 11:11; Luke 7:28). Quite a tribute! No such honor is bestowed on John in the Fourth Gospel. In that latter venue, honor belongs exclusively to Jesus. Even in that setting, there is no escaping the popularity and respect accorded to John by many Jewish people of Palestine at the time of Jesus. The priests and Levites are well aware of it. So they want an answer from John concerning his practice of baptizing Jewish people in the Jordan River. "Why then are you baptizing if you are neither the Messiah, nor Elijah, nor the prophet?" (1:25) Good question. Baptism signals change from an accepted state of being to another; from one way of understanding to another. John's answer is moot, but serving the purpose of the Fourth Evangelist: "I baptize with water. Among you stands one whom you do not know, the one who is coming after me; I am not worthy to untie the thong of his sandal" (1:25–26).

If there was an active community of John the Baptizer still functioning at the time of writing the Fourth Gospel, as seems likely, then the members reading this document would either feel slighted, or convinced that they should transfer their membership from John's community into the community of Jesus Messiah. The rhetoric of the discussion about John as a witness only seems to point in the direction of convincing John's followers to transfer their allegiance over to Jesus, while respecting the witness of John to Jesus when both of them were alive and active in Jewish Palestine.

Further to the subject of "transfer" in chapter 1 is the significant translation of terms going on at the same time. For example, the Aramaic title "Messiah" occurs in two places in the Fourth Gospel (1:41; 4:25), and nowhere else in the New Testament. What I find striking is that the narrator felt obliged to translate the Palestinian Aramaic term, Messiah, into the equivalent "worldwide" Greek term, Christos. This translation of terms in the Fourth Gospel is not merely linguistic, or pedantic. I take it as a "sign" of the development of the early Jesus movement out of its Palestinian locale into the larger Greek-speaking world where the recipients live and work and worship. I have written more substantively on this subject elsewhere.[1]

THE WITNESS URGES THE TRANSFER FROM HIMSELF TO JESUS (3:22–30)

Time now to consider the implicit urging by the Witness to his followers to transfer their allegiance to the greater leader, Jesus. I would urge a close and careful reading of the text of 3:22–30.

Both men practiced baptism as part of their ministry and mission in Jewish Palestine. John chose a place called "Aenon near Salim" because there was plenty of water at that part of the Jordon River. One might construe from this detail that John submerged the candidates fully, although that is not certain. His baptism in the Jordan may have echoed a reenactment of the crossing of the Hebrews into the promised land so many years earlier. Be that as it may, lots of people came to John for baptism. His message must have been compelling. But the specifics of his message are not stated. Clearly, he was popular in his time. He seems to have preached an alternative to the temple and its complicity with Rome. Why else would he call the people out to the river to be baptized? The high priest, resident in Jerusalem, had to be confirmed by the Roman prefect before he could govern the Jewish people. John required no such confirmation from Rome. He simply preached a message that drew many people to him. John's baptism signaled a new way of thinking and living in occupied Palestine. Not much more than that can be said. John's specific message to his converts is not given in the Fourth Gospel. Whatever it was, it drew a crowd to him, and they submitted to the water of Jordan under the urging of this bold, prophetic Jewish figure.

Another observation about the witness of John should be stressed at this point. Among the many who submitted to John's baptism in this

---

1. Shillington, "Significant Translation," 158–70.

Gospel, Jesus is not identified as one of them. Compare that to the testimonial in the Synoptic Gospels. Mark, the earliest of the three, tells about it without equivocation: "Jesus came from Nazareth of Galilee and was baptized by John in the Jordan" (Mark 1:9). Luke follows Mark on this point, adding simply that Jesus was praying as he came up out of the water (3:21). Matthew, by contrast, presents a problem with Jesus being baptized by John. The relevant text reads as follows: "John would have prevented [Jesus], saying, 'I need to be baptized by you, and do you come to me? But Jesus answered him, 'Let it be so now; for it is proper for us in this way to fulfill all righteousness.' Then [John] consented" (Matt 3:14–15). All three Synoptic Gospels attest to the descent of the Spirit on Jesus after his baptism, confirming him as the beloved Son of God.

And the Fourth Gospel attests likewise: "I saw the Spirit descending from heaven like a dove, and it remained on him" (1:32). But that Gospel is singularly mute about Jesus literally being baptized by John. By such silence on the subject, first readers who may not have had access to any of the Synoptic Gospels could easily assume that John the Baptizer did not baptize Jesus. One finds several of these differences in the Fourth Gospel regarding statements and actions present in the Synoptic Gospels, but revised or discarded in the Fourth Gospel. What mattered most to the Fourth Evangelist was that Jesus was imbued with the Spirit of God, and thus qualified to bestow the Holy Spirit on his followers: "He on whom you see the Spirit descend and remain is the one who baptizes with the Holy Spirit" (1:33). That latter baptism matters above all. It transforms the recipient from wrongdoing under God in relation to others, into a holy person under the influence of the Holy Spirit.

Two more brief observations from John's testimony to Jesus will bring this discussion to a close.

First, the Baptizer's call, made twice, to look to Jesus as "the lamb of God who takes away the sin of the world" is rather confusing (1:29, 36). The lamb in Israel, and in later Judaism, was associated with the celebration of Passover. That festival was not one of repentance concerning personal sin and redemption, but one of rejoicing for divine deliverance from external oppression, initially epitomized in the enslavement at the hands of Egyptian overlords. I've heard it said that the lamb in John's vision is more precisely "the ram of atonement with which atonement is made for the guilty party" found in Num 5:8. I find this suggestion less than plausible. I think the allusion to "the sin of the world" may well point to "the world" represented in the egregious politics of Egypt that once enslaved the people of Yahweh. And by extension, then, the over-lordship of Rome may well be in view as "the sin of the world" at the time of John the Baptizer and Jesus. Given this scenario, John hails Jesus as the lamb set forth to take away the oppressive blight of Rome from the Palestinian landscape and its people. I think that notion carries a live possibility.

Atonement for personal sin as well as national sin in Judaism was dealt with on the Day of Atonement (Yom Kippur), the holiest day of the Jewish calendar (tenth of Tishrai, September/October). The people practiced fasting, praying, and refraining from work and pleasure. The ceremony at the time of the temple included the offering of two goats to the priest, one goat dedicated to the Lord and the other to a desert-dwelling demon called Azazel (Lev 16). The goat led out to the wilderness was believed to take away the sin of the people. The ritual is remembered and observed as such to this day in Judaism. So the lamb was not the sin-bearing animal for the Jewish people on the Day of Atonement.

Second, the brief note about John's imprisonment stands out like a boulder in the middle of the discussion about John's popularity with the people of Palestine. One can only wish the narrator would have expanded on the striking interruption in the discussion about many people coming for baptism. There is not a word about John's arrest, or the charge against him. Those two, arrest and charge, seem to me to be significant points for the Fourth Evangelist to make. The political powers of the time, Herod Antipas in Galilee and Pilate with his high priest in Jerusalem, recognized something in John's preaching and baptism that challenged the established mores of the Roman-occupied world. According to the testimony of the Synoptic Gospels, Herod Antipas of Galilee had John beheaded in prison (Mark 6:27; Matt 14:10; Luke 9:9). Whatever the content of John's message, it appears to have threatened the political landscape of the time and place. The Fourth Evangelist is silent about John's execution. Nor does he give a reason for John's imprisonment.[2]

To conclude, I think Rudolf Bultmann made a valid point in his book on the Fourth Gospel when he highlighted a certain rivalry between the disciples of Jesus and the disciples of John the Baptizer. Both groups were baptizing, not merely in the historical timeframe of Jesus and John, but at the time of the composition of the Fourth Gospel at the beginning of the second century. The call of this Gospel, especially in its

---

2. Bultmann, *Gospel of John*, 84–108.

early representation of John the Baptizer as witness to Jesus (chapters 1 and 3), signals to the members of the community living and working in the memory of John to transfer into the community of Jesus the Christ, a transfer that offers nothing less than the kingdom of God through the life and death of Jesus.

4

Anonymous Mother—Nominal Father

THIS IS ANOTHER OF several places in the book where I find it helpful to check in with the three Synoptic Gospels concerning the mother of Jesus, compared to her presence in the Fourth Gospel. After the long history of Christianity, especially with respect to the tradition of Christmas, it scarcely needs comment that the birth and infancy narratives of Matthew and Luke clearly identify the mother of Jesus by name: "Mary." People were given specific names back then, as they are now, by which to identify them in society, and by which others would recognize their personal and social status. It's as simple and as complicated as that.

The mother of Jesus was significant to the framers of the birth narratives in Matthew and Luke, and honored accordingly by declaring her name simply, "Mary." Luke especially signals young Mary's extraordinary talent as the composer of a canticle celebrated to this day under the title, Magnificat (Luke 1:46–55). She was probably fourteen or fifteen when she was engaged to Joseph. Like other young Jewish women of the time and place in history, she would have been barred from formal education. Yet the author of Luke attributed the composition of this wonderful canticle to young Mary.

But what do we find in the Gospel of Mark where no such birth-and-infancy narrative exists? When Jesus speaks out in his hometown the local people recognize him and identify him by his trade, his mother, and his siblings: "Is not this the carpenter, the son of Mary and brother of James and Joses and Judas and Simon, and are not his sisters here with us?" (Mark

6:3). The key observation for our purposes is that the mother of Jesus is identified by her given name, "Mary." His father had probably passed away earlier and is thus not mentioned here, or anywhere else in the Gospel of Mark. Recognizing a person by their proper given name, whether in ancient or modern times, bestows on the person distinctive honor within the society.

We come now to the person of Jesus in relation to his anonymous mother in the Fourth Gospel. Why the author of this Gospel would have left the mother of Jesus nameless is curious. But like all such puzzles, this one prompts attentive readers to raise relevant questions, as I am now doing, in an effort to resolve the quandary. Did the author of the Fourth Gospel not know the name of Jesus's mother? That would be highly unlikely. Did he know her name and unwittingly forgot to include it? That too is very doubtful. More likely at the time of writing the Fourth Gospel at the beginning of the second century CE, the birth narratives of Matthew and Luke were beginning to take hold in the communities of faith in Jesus as Messiah, Son of God. In Matthew and Luke, Mary of Nazareth occupies a prominent place at the beginning of their respective Gospels, especially so in Luke. That is the case because she carried the infant Jesus, acknowledged Son of God, in her womb and delivered him to the world of humankind.

As early as the writings of the apostle Paul in the middle of the first-century Jesus was believed to be uniquely divine. His followers hailed him as Messiah, Son of God for the world. The Fourth Gospel stands in that Pauline tradition, unabashedly declaring the divinity of Jesus from beginning to end. Unlike Jesus in the other three Gospels where he refrains from declaring himself Messiah, Son of God (Mark 8:27–30; Luke 9:18–21), he does so openly in the Fourth Gospel from start to finish. In the opening theological Prologue (1:1–18) the eternal Word (*logos*) becomes flesh in the human person of Jesus, quite apart from any mention of his mother or his birth. Thereafter in the Fourth Gospel Jesus openly enacts divinity in his own words and works. In addition, the super-knowledgeable narrator in this Gospel bolsters what Jesus says and does. This observation relates significantly to the anonymity of the mother of Jesus in this Gospel. Jesus himself bears the image of the invisible God in his own person fully, and independently of his mother's part in carrying him in her womb and delivering him into the world of humankind.

We now know from the historical record of Christianity, following the circulation of the scrolls of Matthew and Luke towards the end of the first century, that the developing church adopted, by simplistic deduction, the doctrine that the mother of Jesus was the "Mother of God." That doctrine did not happen suddenly, much less in a vacuum. Its early manifestation would have circulated variously and incipiently from the beginning of the second century when Matthew and Luke were being read increasingly in Christian communities around the Mediterranean basin. Here, for example, is a second-century interpretation of the angelic announcement to Mary put forward by a revered Christian "defender of the faith," Irenaeus: "The Virgin Mary, being obedient to [God's] word, received from an angel the glad tidings that she would bear God" ("Against Heresies," 5:19:1 [ca. 189 CE]). That deduction, "that she would bear God," effectively endows Mary with very special status. The author of the Fourth Gospel is not prepared to grant that status, presumably because it tends to diminish the supreme and unique significance of the character of Jesus in relation to Creator God the Source of everything: "all things were created by the divine Logos, and apart from that One not a single thing was created that has been created" (1:3).

The main point is this: the writer-compiler of the Fourth Gospel resists the growing notion of his time that Mary should be revered above all other women. As noted above, she is not even granted her proper name in the Fourth Gospel, much less an exalted status as the mother of God. Nor does her son, Jesus, address her as "mother" in this Gospel. Instead, the compiler of this simple-yet-complex Gospel propounds that "it is God the only son, who is close to the Father's heart, who has made [God] known" (1:18), and that without mention of the mediation of Mary who gave birth to Jesus.

It is time now to peruse the three settings in the Fourth Gospel one by one where the mother of Jesus comes to the fore: (1) the dialogue about wedding guests having no wine (2:1–5); (2) "the Jews" cite the father and mother of Jesus against his claim to be "the bread that came down from heaven" (6:41–43; cf. 1:45); (3) Jesus on the cross transfers filial responsibility for his mother to another son (19:25–27). We shall now explore these three texts for insight into the ways in which the mother and father of Jesus are represented.

1. When the wine gave out at a wedding at Cana in Galilee (2:1–5).

Of the several "signs" in the Fourth Gospel, this one about turning water into wine is best known, and much debated. The top question for some debaters is whether the new wine that Jesus made was alcoholic. That one is a nonstarter. The steward who tasted the product Jesus made declares it "good wine," the kind that makes the guests drunk (*methuskō*, 2:9–10). But that is not the focus of our inquiry here. The brief dialogue between Jesus and his mother is the focus.

"The mother of Jesus was there" (2:1). As noted above, this raises a question of identity, especially so for the first readers of this Gospel far removed from the original time and place. Why not "Mary the mother of Jesus" for the uninitiated members of the faith-community located somewhere outside Palestine some sixty to seventy years after the time of Jesus? The issue is one of identity. To suggest that "the mother of Jesus" provides an adequate identity marker is to disavow a long-standing tradition of giving each member of a family a particular name by which to identify themselves in society for the rest of their lives. More importantly, the absence of her proper name reduces her social and communal status. It bears repeating that the second century saw the growing elevation of Mary the mother of Jesus to Mary the mother of God. I think it is safe to infer that the author of the Fourth Gospel knew of the growing theological interest in Mary the mother of Jesus, and refused to include her proper name as a way to accent the unique divinity of Jesus, apart from his mother's conception and delivery of baby Jesus to the world.

We come now to the brief dialogue between Jesus and his mother in this sign-story about a shortage of wine at a wedding. It surprises me that the short dialogue between Jesus and his mother has not received more attention. Perhaps readers have been caught up with the many-sided sign to be bothered with the particulars of the brief dialogue. I think the dialogue, brief as it is, calls for scrutiny by the sheer fact that it is the only dialogue of its kind in the entire Gospel record. The situation at the wedding is grave. The wine gave out, so "the mother of Jesus said to him, 'They have no wine.' And Jesus said to her, 'Woman, what concern is that to you and to me? My hour has not yet come'" (2:3–5).

Two items call for comment: (1) how this brief dialogue about lack of wine at the wedding speaks to the kind of relationship Jesus of the Fourth Gospel had with his mother, and (2) what Jesus meant by "my hour has not yet come."

To the first item. The mother of Jesus may simply be stating a shame-filled fact about the wedding. Wine was and still is a celebrative component at weddings. For the wine to have run dry could render the wedding something of a disaster, shaming the bride and groom. The steward responsible for providing the wine would likewise have lost honor among his friends and employers. The loss of honor in that society was much more serious than it is today, although traces of the honor-shame scenario still exist to some extent in present-day cultures.

Another angle could be that the mother of Jesus was aware of his unusual powers, even though this action is said to be the first sign that Jesus performed. How then could she know what he was capable of doing? Those who promote this motivation in the mother of Jesus, do so with insufficient evidence. Even when she tells the servants to "do whatever he tells you," it does not necessarily imply fabulous powers in Jesus by which he can transform water to wine without it going through the long process of moving up the grapevine and through the process of winemaking. The brief comment from Jesus's mother, "do whatever he tells you," could simply mean that Jesus, familiar with Galilee, will know where the servants might find a winery nearby where they can procure wine. There is nothing in that short text of five English words to prove otherwise. Interpretation should not go too far afield beyond the terms of the text, however tempting it may be to do so.

The critical sentence containing Jesus's response to his mother's comment about the lack of wine is now before us: "Woman, what concern is that to you and to me?" It is hard to treat this brusque question of Jesus to his mother as lovable speech. It comes across as an ancient way of saying, "Woman, mind your own business." I have no doubt that Jesus of Nazareth loved his mother. It's the phrasing in this part of the Fourth Gospel that gives the impression of indifference towards her. What stands out, of course, is the term of address to his mother: "woman." However much some interpreters have tried to generate a pleasant form of address in this expression of Jesus, I am not persuaded, probably because I could never see myself addressing my mother that way. "Woman" (*gunê*) is a generic term indicating a mature female human being. "Mother" (*mêtêr*) is a specific term of filial affection. Why use the generic term? That is the puzzle. It seems to me that the form of address Jesus uses here puts some distance between himself and his mother. She is a woman, not a woman more special than any other woman, and not in any way responsible for the divine character of the human Jesus that comes across boldly in the rest of the Fourth Gospel.

Caution: One has to keep in mind all along the way that the author of the Fourth Gospel is not Jesus, not even in the first-person speeches.

The author behind and within the text is someone committed to honoring the memory of Jesus distinctively and persuasively in this literary form. That includes direct speech in the voice of Jesus. The reality is that Jesus of Nazareth lived and worked some seventy years earlier, spoke Aramaic as a first language, and left behind no firsthand written record of his life and thought.

The second term, "My hour has not yet come," might stop first-time readers of the Fourth Gospel in their tracks. Which "hour" if not this one at Cana? The reader has to keep reading to find out. The grammatical phrasing occurs five times in the narrative context while Jesus is performing signs (2:4; 7:6; 7:8; 7:30; 8:20). When the sign-narratives are finished at the end of chapter 11, and the Passion discourses are underway, the tense of the verb changes from "not yet come" to "has come" (12:23; 17:1). In short, the hour towards which Jesus moves in the Fourth Gospel is when he lays down his life for the salvation of others in the world. At that point, God honors the work of Jesus in the world, and glorifies him singularly, not because of a biological relationship to his mother (16:14; 17:1; 17:5). From the time of her brief dialogue with Jesus in chapter 2, including a brief rendezvous in Capernaum (2:12), the mother of Jesus does not appear again in his presence until the time of his crucifixion reported in chapter 19, discussed below.

2. "The Jews" point to both the father and mother of Jesus against his claim to be "the bread that came down from heaven" (6:41–43; cf. 1:45).

The nametag, "the Jews," is unfortunate in the Fourth Gospel. I have devoted a separate chapter below to the implications of the use of this term in this Gospel. For now, I am interested in the way this group calls up the parents as evidence against the claim Jesus makes about his origin and his life-giving grace symbolized by bread from heaven. The text is short enough to quote here in full for clarity.

> Then the Jews began to complain about him because he said, "I am the bread that came down from heaven." They were saying, "Is not this Jesus, the son of Joseph, whose father and mother we know? How can he now say, 'I have come down from heaven'?" Jesus answered them, "Do not complain among yourselves. No one can

Anonymous Mother—Nominal Father

come to me unless drawn by the Father who sent me; and I will raise that person up on the last day." (6:41–44)

The point of interest arises out of the two rhetorical questions put forward within earshot of Jesus. The event that prompted the debate was the sign in which Jesus provided enough bread from five barley loaves to feed about five thousand people. Five thousand is a huge number of hungry people gathered at any time and place in history. How much more so in the small country of Palestine in the first century. But Jesus expounded the need for symbolic bread from heaven to sustain the human spirit. This discourse about the bread of life is the longest in the Fourth Gospel, comprising seventy-one verses in all.

In the middle of this longest speech of Jesus about the significance of the sign of providing bread to the hungry, we find a sign of disbelief resulting in two questions focusing the subject under review here. The two questions are related. Both have to do with the earthly origin and identity of Jesus. "Is not this Jesus, the son of Joseph, whose father and mother we know? How can he now say, 'I have come down from heaven'?"

Consider the ramification of the first of these two questions: "Is not this Jesus, the son of Joseph, whose father and mother we know?" This is the only Gospel that identifies the earthly Jesus as "the son of Joseph" without further qualification (cf. Luke 3:23). What I find striking is that the mother of Jesus is also present in the question, but once again nameless. It seems to be yet another moment in this Gospel where the significance given to the mother of Jesus in Matthew and Luke is diminished. Instead, the father of Jesus is honored and identified here by name, with the mother placed in second position. It may be argued, of course, that the problem of Joseph as the father of Jesus appears here in the voice of unbelieving "Jews," thereby rendering their verdict incorrect and invalid. That might have merit if this were the only place in this Gospel where Joseph appears as the father of Jesus. But that is not so. As early as chapter 1, a loyal disciple of Jesus affirms Joseph as the father of Jesus. Here is the text for reference. "Now Philip was from Bethsaida, the city of Andrew and Peter. Philip found Nathanael and said to him, "We have found him about whom Moses in the law and also the prophets wrote, Jesus son of Joseph from Nazareth" (1:45).

Several observations come to light here. Philip was already a disciple of Jesus when he met up with Nathanael; Philip is trying to persuade Nathanael to become a follower of Jesus; Philip hailed from the same city as

Andrew and Peter. Consider the last observation first. Both Andrew and Peter were well-recognized disciples of Jesus, and Philip lived in the same town, and presumably knew the two notable disciples. Given this scenario for understanding the identity of Jesus in the voice of Philip, he then tells Nathanael that Jesus is the son of Joseph from Nazareth. But what is even more poignant, or disturbing, is the total absence of the mother of Jesus from Philip's dialogue with Nathanael about the identity of Jesus. One would expect from Philip some credit given to the mother of Jesus for bearing this son, Jesus. That is all the more pressing considering the likelihood that Joseph had already died before that time, while the mother of Jesus was still alive.

I think these queries can be resolved to some degree at least, by recognizing the situation in the life of the faith community at the time of writing this Fourth Gospel on the threshold of the second century. It seems the author is not prepared to afford the mother of Jesus a position of honor that would jeopardize in any way the singular significance of Jesus as unique Son of God without recourse to his mother's role in his being born into the world. We come now to the last striking interface between Jesus and his mother.

3. Jesus on the cross transfers filial responsibility for his mother to another son (19:25–27).

It may seem odd to cite a story in Luke 7 as a point of entry into a very significant moment between Jesus and his mother while his life is slowly passing from his body. But this story from Luke is relevant to the words Jesus utters from the cross to his mother.

> [Jesus] went to a town called Nain . . . As he approached the gate of the town, a man who had died was being carried out. He was his mother's only son, and she was a widow; and with her was a large crowd from the town. When the Lord saw her, he had compassion for her and said to her, "Do not weep." Then he came forward and touched the bier, and the bearers stood still. And he said, "Young man, I say to you, rise!" The dead man sat up and began to speak, and Jesus gave him to his mother. (Luke 7:11–15)

This striking story illustrates the social reality that there was no government-sponsored welfare system in the first-century Holy Land. If a widowed mother had a family, especially sons, she would fare quite well.

It was culturally incumbent on sons to care for a widowed mother. In this story from Luke 7, a mother's only son had died. Doubtless, the mother was mourning her son's death. But she also weeps in her heart about the loss of her livelihood. Remember there was no social network to provide for the lone widow. At the death of her only son she was at the mercy of neighbors and friends who may or may not help her. This dead man was her *only* son. If she had other sons they would take over the responsibility in the event of an older son's death. Aware of that social situation, Jesus remedies it by restoring her son to her. Now she is assured of a livelihood.

Compare that to the situation at the time and place of the death of Jesus. The mother of Jesus is still alive and present at the foot of the cross. What will happen to her in the aftermath of Jesus's death? This is where the story differs from the one in Luke 7. The mother of Jesus had five sons, including her firstborn, Jesus. We find the list of given names of four sons—other than Jesus—in Mark 6. It is safe to assume that the order of the names on the list is from the oldest to the youngest: James and Joses and Judas and Simon. So the mother of Jesus is much more secure economically and socially than the widow of Nain of Luke 7. It's probably plain to see where this line of reasoning is going. But I am going to leave it there for now, to be recaptured in a later chapter devoted to the loving relationship Jesus had with one particular disciple.

We return now to the interface between Jesus and his mother at the time of his death in Jerusalem. Here is the salient text from chapter 19 of the Fourth Gospel: "When Jesus saw his mother and the disciple whom he loved standing beside her, he said to his mother, 'Woman, here is your son.' Then he said to the disciple, 'Here is your mother.' And from that hour the disciple took her into his own home" (19:26–27). This has the ring of a socially recognized transfer of responsibility in the presence of several witnesses. Once more we have Jesus addressing his mother: "Woman, here is your son." It may have been a custom in that society for a son to address his mother in this way. Contemporary evidence for such address is sparse. I doubt it would go down well today. The word of address, in this case, is two-pronged. First, Jesus addresses his mother, then the man at the foot of the cross, "Here is your mother." At that point the mother of Jesus is assured of a place to live, and sustenance for living by the hand of this second son.

In closing this chapter I point more broadly to the motif of anonymity in the Fourth Gospel. We found it evident each time the mother of Jesus entered the narrative. Her name was not given even once. The other striking case of anonymity in this Gospel comes through in the second part in connection with one disciple in particular, known only as "the disciple whom Jesus loved." I have no doubt that Jesus loved his mother as well. That factor is represented at the end of Jesus's earthly life when he transfers the well-being of his mother to another son. The love Jesus had for that one disciple in particular now goes through him to his mother. This specific case will come under closer scrutiny again in a later chapter.

ADDENDUM

A word of caution is in order about honoring the primary terms of the text. Anonymity is deliberate in the Fourth Gospel, not an oversight. The urge to come up with proper names in each case, either from post-biblical tradition or from modern sermons, vitiates the literary ploy of anonymity. Better to try to understand the element of anonymity in context, and leave it at that. Hence, an English version of the Bible produced by a qualified committee of scholars is preferable over a paraphrase produced by a single individual. The New Revised Standard Version (NRSV) that I use throughout the book serves the purpose rather well. The aim is to hold prejudice in check in an effort to make the interpretation authentic.

5

Two Inquisitive Neighbors: Different as Night and Day

IT'S HARDLY A COINCIDENCE that two very different individuals have a chapter devoted to each of them side-by-side in the Fourth Gospel. A distinguished Jewish male scholar named Nicodemus gets the floor to put some leading questions to Jesus in the opening dialogue of chapter 3, while an anonymous woman of questionable reputation holds her own with Jesus beside an iconic well in her country of Samaria in chapter 4. The Jewish man comes to Jesus under cover of darkness; the Samaritan woman appears in broad daylight at noon.

There can be no mistaking the deliberate use of irony within and between these two chapters. The well-known ancient philosopher, Socrates (470–399 BCE), used the ironic question method to prove his debater wrong and himself right. Nicodemus may fall under that ironic canopy, to some degree at least. Likewise the woman of Samaria. Yet there is more to irony in the Fourth Gospel than the Socratic method of doing philosophy. One of the differences between Nicodemus's questions to Jesus and those of the Samaritan woman is that Nicodemus planned his question period with Jesus, while the woman's encounter was completely unplanned. Nonetheless, her questions were even more probing.

Irony at heart is a contra-method of teaching and learning: physical birth against Spirit-birth (chapter 3) and well water against Spirit-water (chapter 4). But there is a much broader aspect of ironic literary education going on between the two chapters. In chapter 3, debater Nicodemus is well-educated, well-respected, and able to teach within his Jewish community. In chapter 4 the woman at the well in Samaria has no such qualifications. Ironically she grasps the insightful message of Jesus, and goes back to her village to teach her fellow Samaritans. And they believe her, and make their way to Jesus with a bold confession: "we know that this is truly the Savior of the world" (4:42). Moreover, broad-spectrum irony lies in the positioning of the two contra-stories side-by-side, with the unlikely woman of Samaria winning the day over the respected man of Judea. Irony is present elsewhere in this Gospel, but this one tops the lot, as far as I can see. For more on the conceit of irony, consult Paul D. Duke, *Irony in the Fourth Gospel*.

Time now to probe some particulars of the two debates coming to us in the "voices" of the respective debaters facing off with Jesus in chapters 3 and 4.

WHEN TWO JEWISH RABBIS DEBATE WITHIN THE SPECTRUM OF TEMPLE JUDAISM

It bears repeating that two time frames, with their two cultural situations, converge in the Fourth Gospel. One is the implied time and situation of the narrative depicting the last few years of Jesus's life and ministry in Palestine up to and including his crucifixion in 30 CE, what I call here "the spectrum of Temple Judaism." The other is the time and situation in the life and thought of the author as he recreates the story for his community living about seventy years after the death of Jesus, thirty years after the downfall of the powerful temple of Jerusalem. These two frames of reference merge invariably, but not overtly in the narrative. It is up to the attentive reader-interpreter to identify the literary-theological intertwining of these two temporal-cultural frames as far as possible. By doing so the message of the book becomes full-bodied rather than truncated.

What did it mean at the time and place of Jesus to be a Pharisee? It is not uncommon to hear modern Christian leaders berate all Pharisees as narrow-minded, self-righteous, critics of everybody else but themselves. The aim of such an attack, so it seems, is to warn the Christian congregation against becoming such hypocritical people in religious garb. That caricature of all Pharisees in the first century is unbecoming for a genuine Christian spirit on the one hand, and lacking in historical understanding on the other. If only we could ask a real Pharisee like Nicodemus of the first century how he understood himself under that denominational label. No mistake here: I did mean denominational. To call the Pharisees a "sect" of Judaism, as is often done, sends an implicit signal immediately that every member of the group is self-absorbed and self-righteous. The English spelling of "Pharisee" comes directly from Greek, but that Greek term has its root in the Aramaic, *prīšayyā*. Its plural means "separated ones." It was a positive term in Judaism at the time of Jesus. The Pharisees distinguished themselves by their ardent commitment to God's holy Law (Torah). They believed that the Law was binding on all the people of Israel claiming relationship to Israel's Lord.

The same "separated ones" believed themselves called to ensure that the people of God knew the Law in order to observe it in everyday life. Hence their use of the title Rav, or Rabbi, "Teacher." It is worth noting that our story opens with the Pharisee, Nicodemus, referring to Jesus as "Rabbi." This Nicodemus recognizes the ministry of Jesus as authentic, without prejudice or sarcasm: "Rabbi, we [Pharisees] know that you are a teacher who has come from God" (3:2).

EXCURSUS

It bears mentioning that the Pharisees were not the only identifiable group within temple Judaism. First-century Jewish historian Josephus identifies three other groups by their title and description. One was the Essenes, who cast a cold eye on temple religion of the time, and withdrew from temple worship. They adopted their own form of worship and teaching, far away from Jerusalem, and identified themselves openly as the Jewish faithful while rejecting the high priest of the temple. Their sharp critique of the temple priesthood probably sprang from the close alignment of the high priest with the Roman prefect who had the final say in temple politics. The Essenes of Josephus's description appear to be represented in the archaeological remains of a community located on the northwest corner of the Dead Sea, far away from Jerusalem and temple. The people who occupied the site were devout copyists and writers, evidenced in the extant scrolls known today as the Dead Sea Scrolls.

The people in the third major Jewish group cited by Josephus were known as Sadducees. These were likewise a recognizable group whose primary interest was temple ritual and sacrifice. The high priest and other priests serving the temple were drawn from this Jewish group. Sadducees were rather more aristocratic than the other groups. They did not believe in the resurrection, as the Pharisees did, nor did they put much stock in the oral tradition of Judaism. Their religious and theological focus was on the five scrolls of the Law. Teachings outside the Law scrolls were without authority, according to the Sadducees. The duties of this Jewish group of Sadducees came to an end with the destruction of the temple in 70 CE. They were not heard from again as a group.

There was also another band of Jewish revolutionaries known as Zealots. They believed themselves to be called of God to defend the traditions and the temple of Judaism against ungodly forces from the outside. Their militaristic theology drew many to their side, especially when the Roman militia invaded Palestine in 66 CE. The Zealots believed that if they fought against the alien forces in the name of God they would win the battle in God's name and by God's power. That ideological posture proved to be unsound.

By 70 CE Jerusalem and its temple were devastated, the Sadducees and the Essenes vanquished, as also the Zealot group. The only recognizable group that survived the holocaust of 66–70 CE in Palestine was that of the Pharisees. The Romans allowed the Pharisees to set up house in the city of Jamnia in Gaza, far away from the Holy City and the Temple Mount. The term "Pharisees" soon disappeared in the aftermath of destruction, to be replaced by "Rabbis." And behold Rabbinic Judaism was born, and remains as such to this day.[3]

The recognizable groups of Jewish leaders, identified above, were small in number compared to another Jewish group, also identified by Josephus: "people of the land." These Jewish peasants of Galilee and Judea were far more numerous than all the special groups put together. The rabbis in post-temple Judaism continued in their role as leaders and teachers of the Jewish people of the land. Extant Jewish literature, especially the Mishnah and Talmud, bears testimony to the diligence and conviction of the rabbis in preserving the traditions of Judaism for generations to follow. The author of the Fourth Gospel seems to be aware of the presence and effectiveness of this renewed Judaism led by the rabbinic survivors of the Roman invasion of Jewish Palestine, including especially the destruction of the Jewish temple.

Returning now to the ironic dialogue between Nicodemus the Pharisee and Jesus the Nazarene, let us explore the give-and-take between the

---

3. Martyn, *History and Theology*.

two teachers to the point where it becomes a monologue in the voice of Jesus alone.

Nicodemus puts forward a glowing report coming from his group of respected teachers: "Rabbi [Jesus], we know that you are a teacher who has come from God; for no one can do these signs that you do apart from the presence of God" (3:2). That kind of endorsement deserves a response along the line of "Thank you. Glad you approve." Instead, Jesus responds with a far-out metaphor that throws Nicodemus into disarray. "Very truly, I tell you," says Jesus, "no one can see the kingdom of God without being born from above"(3:3). If the same statement came in the voice of an evangelical pastor today, the audience would nod immediately in approval without question. They seem to know what it means without further ado, and are ready at a moment's notice to convince anyone who needs to make a decision to put their trust in Jesus. But alas, the metaphor is not about human decision-making one way or another. To use the metaphor in such a way is to undercut its pungent and provocative power. No wonder the educated Nicodemus has a few questions for Jesus, as all of us should.

First question: "How can anyone be born after having grown old?" (3:4a). That is not a trick question. Nicodemus, like every human being before or after him, knows full well that every human being is subject to disease, aging and dying. There is no physical rebirth before or after death. His second question makes Jesus's assertion about rebirth sound absurd. "Can one enter a second time into the mother's womb and be born?" (3:4b). Totally absurd! So there has to be another way of understanding the statement of Jesus about being "born from above," or being "born again." The Greek word is *anōthen*. It's a bit ambiguous, and therefore subject to various translations into English. It could mean, "born again," as in a sequence. But the more likely inference from *anōthen* is "from above": new life comes from a higher realm than the physical, human inclination to reproduce a flesh-and-blood human being in their likeness without the offspring's approval to do so.

Jesus goes on to explain before Nicodemus utters his last question. The main subject is the kingdom of God. How does one prepare for life in the kingdom rule of God? There are no easy answers. The answer Jesus gives is laden with mystery. Birth from above happens by water-and-Spirit, he says. Water baptism may be in view, as the ending of chapter 3 implies. I have hyphenated the three words because water and Spirit are tightly tied together in the Fourth Gospel. Water is unambiguously life-giving for every single organism under the sun: plant, animal, and human. Beyond this earthly sphere, the equivalent life-giving power is Spirit. Both are givens. That is, the two exist quite apart from any human ingenuity, and are absolutely needed for conscious life. Nicodemus misses that point, it seems. But Jesus continues to drive the point home in any case. "Do not be astonished that I said to you, 'You must be born from above.' The wind blows where it chooses, and you hear the sound of it, but you do not know where it comes from or where it goes. So it is with everyone who is born of the Spirit" (3:7–8). There it is.

The human mind and body should not, must not, try to bring about birth from above. That sphere of being is beyond human influence or inclination. If we are honest with ourselves we will admit we had nothing to do with our being born into the physical world in the first place. Why would we then think we are in full control of being born from above into the kingdom of God? The wind blows and we cannot stop it. It ceases and we cannot make it blow. We can't see the wind, but we know its presence. We feel its power. We take it into our lungs without deciding to do so, and it gives us life. That is the metaphor for birth from above. No wonder Nicodemus asks his third and final question: "How can these things be?" (3:9). It is out of our hands, Nicodemus, however much we humans like to think along the line of Frank Sinatra's song, "I did it my way."

Jesus closes out the conversation with Nicodemus with a question of his own, and not a very sympathetic one. "Are you a teacher of Israel, and yet you do not understand these things?" (3:10). The question is somewhat critical, and falls somewhat short of many-splendored love. I would venture to say that the dialogue Jesus had with Nicodemus reflects the kind of banter that was going on between the new people of Jesus Messiah and the new community of Jewish rabbis centered in Jamnia in the post-temple period. The Jewish rabbinic leaders worked hard to consolidate a renewed Judaism around the world in the absence of the temple. The new community of Jesus, at the same time, had begun to take root around the Mediterranean basin, and continued to engage in mission in the name of Jesus. Creative tension between the two fledgling communities of faith, even though both were rooted in historic Judaism, led to the breakdown of sympathetic understanding between them.

At verse 11 of chapter 3 the tone changes. The dialogue between the two rabbis shifts from one-on-one singular to group-plural: "we" and "you." The plural "you" is scarcely noticed in modern English, because "you" in modern English can be understood as singular or plural, depending on context. Only the context in English determines the number, but that context is often veiled. In the King James Version of 1611 "ye," the plural form of "you" singular, was still in use. At any rate, here is how the dialogue between Jesus and Nicodemus shifts away from dialogue to monologue on the part of Jesus, leaving Nicodemus in the shadows for a while. He appears again briefly in chapter 7 where he defends Jesus against the scrutiny of the Pharisees (7:50–52), and finally when he and Joseph of Arimathea expedite the temporary burial of the crucified Jesus (19:38–42). Meanwhile, take note in the text below that every highlighted "you" is plural, as in "you all." The singular Nicodemus is no longer in focus, but rather the whole group of Jewish rabbis that Nicodemus represents:

> Very truly, I tell *you*, we speak of what we know and testify to what we have seen; yet *you* do not receive our testimony. If I have told *you* about earthly things and *you* do not believe, how can *you* believe if I tell *you* about heavenly things? . . . For God so loved the world that he gave his only Son, so that everyone who believes in him may not perish but may have eternal life. (3:11–16)

As I reread that text, I find myself obliged to believe that "the world" God loves includes that part of the world occupied by Nicodemus and his fellow Jewish rabbis in every generation.

JESUS MEETS A SAMARITAN WOMAN BESIDE AN ICONIC WELL

It would be helpful to have an image of the geographical boundaries of first-century Palestine on hand at this juncture. An internet map of Palestine serves the purpose quite well. Judea, where Jesus talked with Nicodemus, lies in the southern part of Palestine, west of the Dead Sea and the Jordan River. The region of Galilee, the name of the territory where Jesus grew up and later ministered publicly, is situated in the northern part of the country on the west side of the Jordan River. Between those two areas of land, Galilee to the north and Judea to the south, is the territory of Samaria in the middle of Palestine. It would be unusual to find a devout Jewish citizen or Jewish slave rubbing shoulders with Samaritans at the time of Jesus. As our narrator adroitly points out, "the Jews have no dealings with the Samaritans" (4:9 KJV).

Centuries earlier a significant number of the northern tribes of Israel set up their political center in the ancient city of Shechem—Sychar of the Fourth Gospel; modern West Bank city of Nablus—between Mount Gerizim to the south and Mount Ebal to the north. In due course, the Assyrian king captured the Israelite inhabitants of Samaria and carried them off to Assyria (2 Kgs 15–23). When the dust settled some years later, and the Assyrian regime weakened, a remnant returned to Samaria with latent memories of their history, and not least a copy of their version of the Law scrolls of Moses. The Samaritans, as they were called at the time of Jesus, reestablished themselves around the sacred site of Sychar between the two mountains. The well that Jacob gave to his son Joseph is still there providing water. At least it was there when a group of us visitors stopped for a drink some years ago. Sure enough, the well is deep and the water cold.

Stories about the resettlement of a remnant of the northern tribes of Israel in Samaria after the exile of the northern tribes are mixed, and not especially germane to our investigation of the theme of love running through the story about Jesus and the Samaritan woman at the well, to which we now give attention.

Before pursuing the details of the encounter Jesus had with a Samaritan woman, there remains a further query about his trip from Judea to Galilee. First, the stated motive behind Jesus's decision to leave Judea and go to Galilee was that the Pharisees had learned that he was baptizing more disciples than John the Baptizer (4:1). Why that would be a problem for the Pharisees at the time of Jesus is not obvious from the text. Second, it is stated, "he had to go through Samaria" (4:4). I have heard it said in sermons that Jesus knew in advance that a Samaritan woman needed his word of grace and encouragement. Hence his decision to go through her country. But that strains the logic of the text at that point in the story. The statement has more to do with the configuration of the geography. Literally, it was *logically* expedient for him to go through Samaria, rather than go all the way around it, as devout Jewish people might do. Implicitly, then, his decision to go through the questionable territory of Samaria was counterintuitive and countercultural, but logically correct. It was this kind of thinking and acting that ultimately led the authorities in Jerusalem to take steps against the ministry of Jesus, especially so in Judea.

The story of Jesus's encounter with a woman of Samaria is rather well-known to a cross-section of people. So, rather than go into elaborate detail, I shall highlight a few features that appear to me to warrant scrutiny and reflection. By the time Jesus reached the well that Jacob gave to his son Joseph, he was parched and tired. It was midday and presumably hot. Jesus had neither a bucket nor a rope. The well was deep. Then along comes a woman with a bucket, and a heart full of questions. Jesus asks her for a drink of water from the historic well.

"How is it that you, a Jew, ask a drink of me, a woman of Samaria?" the woman asks. In response, Jesus becomes as enigmatic as he was with Nicodemus. Enigma has a way of making a person think differently, maybe even change their way of thinking and acting. Jesus speaking now: "If you knew the gift of God, and who it is that is saying to you, 'Give me a drink,' you would have asked him, and he would have given you living water" (4:10). It's easy for modern Christians to hear those words and carry on as usual. They have heard sermons on the text. But when one imagines standing to listen to that language of Jesus for the very first time it is, to say the least, far out! Who ever heard of "living water"? The woman is actually well acquainted with the history of the place. Jesus is a stranger to her. His words are strange to her. Her response is actually very astute. "Are you greater than our ancestor Jacob, who gave us the well, and with his sons and his flocks drank from it?" (4:12) Instead of saying a simple "Yes," Jesus announces yet another mystery that the woman fails to understand. How could she understand? Jesus is still talking about water. This woman knows water. She comes to the well regularly, glad to have a well that endlessly gives her fresh water.

But Jesus goes one better than the well water, good as it is. Imagine being in the woman's shoes hearing these words for the very first time. "Everyone who drinks of this water will be thirsty again, but those who drink of the water that I will give them will never be thirsty. The water that I will give will become in them a spring of water gushing up to eternal life." The woman doesn't quite get it. "Sir, give me this water, so that I may never be thirsty or have to keep coming here to draw water" (4:14–15). Instead of explaining his cryptic saying about "living water" that will quench thirst permanently, Jesus unabashedly pries into the woman's social-ethical life. "Go, call your husband, and come back," Jesus said, knowing all the while that she previously had five husbands. And the current man in her life was not "husband" in the cultural-religious sense (4:16–18). Many a person would have walked away from such inquiry and critique. But this woman stood her ground. She turned the topic to their respective religions.

"Our ancestors worshipped on this mountain, but you say that the place where people must worship is in Jerusalem" (4:20). Again, Jesus critiques her Samaritan religion in favor of Judaism. "You worship what you do not know; we worship what we know, for salvation is from the Jews" (4:22). But then he qualifies the restriction to any one religion, even his own religion of Judaism. What follows is one of the most telling statements of faith, applicable to all variations of the human family, to every culture and nationality. As I ponder this grand profession from the heart and mind of Jesus I take courage. A particular name of a religion, a particular name for the Creator of the universe, is set aside. In its place, we have this cosmic vision of Jesus. Every one of us should ponder it well. Discuss it together. Think of its ramifications for the human family. It overcomes the human urge to think of our own particular culture and religion as the only acceptable identity to have in the whole world. Here it is: "But the hour is coming, and is now here, when the true worshipers will worship the Father in spirit and truth, for the Father seeks such as these to worship him. God is spirit, and those who worship [God] must worship in spirit and truth" (4:23–24).

Here are some pointers to ponder. True worshipers are not locked into one form of worship, and one way of understanding the Creator-Sustainer of the universe. The metaphor for the divine Spirit is "Father," with the assumption that "Father" signals provider, guardian, and lover of his offspring. And finally "God is Spirit," neither a place nor a building nor a creedal statement nor a material symbol of any sort. "God is Spirit," and thereby accessible to every human spirit in search of meaning and true life.

We could sign off on the discussion of Jesus in a Samaritan context at this point. But there is one more query niggling at my mind before leaving the story about Samaria, the woman who gave Jesus a drink, and the ones who made a bold confession in relation to Jesus. Here is the query: What are we to make of the out-of-context interjection in brackets in the NRSV as follows?

> When the two days were over, he went from that place to Galilee (for Jesus himself had testified that a prophet has no honor in the prophet's own country). When he came to Galilee, the Galileans welcomed him, since they had seen all that he had done in Jerusalem at the festival; for they too had gone to the festival. (4:43–45)

The cluster of words in parenthesis simply does not fit within the surrounding text. At one level it reads as though Samaria was Jesus's own country where he had no honor, hence his need to go to Galilee after two days in Samaria. But Samaria was not "his own country," so that route is a dead-end. He was treated rather well in Samaria in any case. Perhaps, then, Galilee is the country in view in the bracketed statement. He had lived in the village

Two Inquisitive Neighbors: Different as Night and Day

of Nazareth in Galilee for more than a quarter of a century, and traveled throughout the region. So after the two days in Samaria Jesus set out for his familiar home territory, Galilee. Suddenly that simple comment about his journey north is qualified in the strangest way imaginable: "for Jesus himself had testified that a prophet has no honor in the prophet's own country." Is that why Jesus set out for Galilee, because he, being a prophet, would not be honored there? That seems odd. Stranger still, immediately after the parenthetical comment Jesus did indeed reach Galilee where the Galilean people received him honorably.

So the saying is simply out of context in this part of the Fourth Gospel. The author presumably picked up the saying of Jesus recorded in Mark 6:4. In that text Jesus had come to his hometown and his own people of Nazareth specifically, the village where he had lived for about twenty-five years. As reported in Mark 6, when he returned to his home village as a preacher and teacher the village people were puzzled by his new mode of speech, and they failed to support him. So Jesus pronounced the proverb in that specific village setting: "Prophets are not without honor, except in their hometown, and among their own kin, and in their own house" (Mark 6:4; par. Matt. 13:54–57; Luke 4:24). The setting in the Fourth Gospel is different. Jesus is leaving Samaria to go to Galilee, not specifically Nazareth. And "when [Jesus] came to Galilee, the Galileans welcomed him, since they had seen all that he had done in Jerusalem at the festival; for they too had gone to the festival." Accordingly, Jesus the prophet was welcomed and respected by the Galileans when he arrived. No wonder the translators of the NRSV decided to enclose the out-of-context proverb in brackets.

6

The Brothers

JESUS HAD BIOLOGICAL BROTHERS. To argue otherwise is to skew their literary presence in every Gospel of the canonical four. Motivation for such an unbecoming argument is not hard to find. In post-New Testament times, church councils and resulting creeds became the touchstone for theological understanding and rock-solid confessions of faith. The councilor statements and ensuing creeds and confessions then functioned as the means by which to read the texts of the New Testament. Creeds, however magisterial, act as fixed forms of Christian faith, and as such they tend to stifle responsible interpretation of the complex character of biblical texts. Interpretation of historical biblical texts should speak authentically out of an original text-in-context frame, and thence into new situations in life. That endeavor—as I have learned through many years of study and teaching—is not as easy as it appears on this page. One of my mentors said more than once many years ago, "authenticity is the heart of the matter."[4] And I agree completely. But achieving that worthy quality takes courage, discipline, and self-awareness.

Here is a classic example of a later confessional stance with respect to the brothers of Jesus. They were not really biological brothers, because Mary bore only Jesus, the Son of God. Giving birth to other children would make Mary impure by engaging in sexual relations with a human male, namely her husband Joseph. This belief springs from a later doctrine about the immaculate conception of Mary herself, which in turn led to the sinless, virginal conception of the Son of God. And Mary remained immaculate

---

4. Meyer, *Critical Realism*, 45.

virgin for the rest of her life. So where does this leave the "brothers" of Jesus presented as such in the four Gospels? Answer: they were biological children of Joseph from a previous marriage. Then through Joseph's "marriage" to Mary they were *called* brothers of Jesus, but they were really stepbrothers of Jesus. There are variations on this scenario. But this well-known one serves to illustrate how later doctrinal positions affect how we read and interpret the respective texts of each of the four Gospels.

I have set up the above paragraphs to help catch ourselves when we, unwittingly, resort to established creeds and traditions from a later time through which to understand particular biblical texts in their own cultural time frame. That inclination and action leads to an ill-conceived prooftext approach. Prooftexting too often becomes a way to keep within creedal boundaries. By prooftexting I mean bringing together a few texts that look and feel the same, while ignoring others that don't. I shall leave it at that for the present purpose, even though the subject is worthy of much more weighty discussion. In short, I am trying in these chapters to represent the tone and texture of various aspects of the Fourth Gospel. By so doing I hope to generate some new and true insight into this distinctive Gospel in the New Testament.

Time now to turn attention to the brothers of Jesus as they come across in the Fourth Gospel, supplemented by their portrayal in two other sources in the New Testament: Paul's letters and the Acts of the Apostles.

We find the brothers in *three settings* in the Fourth Gospel. I shall deal with each one in turn.

A FEW DAYS' STOPOVER AT CAPERNAUM IN GALILEE

Immediately following the narrative about the wedding in Cana of Galilee we come upon a short, yet illuminating note about a group that gathered at the town of Capernaum. Here's how it reads. "After this [Jesus] went down to Capernaum with his mother, his brothers, and his disciples; and they remained there a few days" (2:12). That is the full extent of the description of what appears to be a pleasant little holiday with friends and family for a few days. We can only wish we had been there in such a jocund company following the wedding at Cana. I can only imagine how the conversation might have moved along as they ate together reclining around the table, walking together down the dusty roads, talking to the townspeople, and wandering through the fields where sheep were safely grazing. But this is neither a novel nor a poem, so I dare not move further in that direction. The information we do have from this brief narrative is striking. Here are some observations.

The focus, as one might expect, is on Jesus. He has already begun to speak and act in ways that challenge his Jewish counterparts to rethink their Jewish hope for independence in the face of Roman imperial occupation. As far as we can tell, for Jesus the approach should not be to stand guard over the long-standing heritage of Israel. Instead he announced a new kind of kingdom, unlike that of King David or King Solomon or King Augustus of Rome: a kingdom that has its life and energy coming from above. He says as much to a leading Jewish rabbi, Nicodemus. "I tell you, no one can see the kingdom of God without being born from above" (3:3). But Jesus did not reject his Jewish parents nor his commitment to the Jewish covenant represented in the Hebrew Scriptures. That observation is not always welcome within some Christian circles to this day.

I have heard it said variously in churches that Jesus created a new way to God, *over against* the Judaism of his day. I view the ministry of Jesus, instead, to be one of radical renewal of Jewish life and thought and attitude. He was generating a new frontier for understanding his Jewish heritage, not conspiring to bring about its demise. On the contrary, he was reconstituting his Jewish heritage as a spiritual reality in the land that speaks to the needs of the people and the culture of the time. The Fourth Gospel is the most radical of the four in its way of putting that vision of Jesus forward.

Again, we can only imagine the conversations that went on during those few days in Capernaum. Consider the people present. Jesus is there of course. His mother and brothers are with him, and not least his student-followers. I wonder what the mother of Jesus might have said. Would she have warned her son not to go too far with his grand vision of the kingdom of God? I can imagine her trying to protect her son from imprisonment, or death at the hands of the political power brokers, such as Herod Antipas, ruler of Galilee. Such political power brokers do not brook opposition to their regime. I think his brothers might have suggested caution, without abandoning Jesus's vision altogether. I can imagine the disciples saying little, being still learners at the feet of rabbi Jesus.

One rather inconspicuous word comes up in this brief text: "remained." Actually, its Greek form occurs numerous times in this Gospel, translated variously as "remain," "stay," or "abide." This variation in English translation tends to cloud the significance of the word in Greek. But when we encounter chapter 15 we find one of these three English words hitting us between the eyes: "abide." It occurs no less than ten times in ten verses in chapter 15. The inconspicuous appearance of the word in the earlier chapters suddenly takes on a very serious note at chapter 15. It seems that some confessions of faith in Jesus vaporize after a while. When that happens the person loses out on the life-giving grace of God in Jesus. In practical terms, members in the particular community represented in this Fourth Gospel had probably come under pressure from one side or another, so that some were leaving the group. The urgency in this Gospel is to stay, remain, abide. That's the key to the saving grace of God. So the group of disciples, brothers, mother, and Jesus *remain* together for a few days. Life comes from true community that never gives up, and never breaks up.

THE BROTHERS WANT BROTHER JESUS TO GO TO THE FESTIVAL OF BOOTHS WITH THEM

The situation under review here, and the festive event associated with it, is one of the most confusing scenarios in the entire Fourth Gospel. The text in focus really needs to be set out in plain view to facilitate a modicum of understanding.

> The Jewish festival of Booths was near. So his brothers said to [Jesus], "Leave here and go to Judea so that your disciples also may see the works you are doing; for no one who wants to be widely known acts in secret. If you do these things, show yourself to the world." (For not even his brothers believed in him.) Jesus said to them, "My time has not yet come, but your time is always here . . . Go to the festival yourselves. I am not going to this festival, for my time has not yet fully come." After saying this, he remained in Galilee. But after his brothers had gone to the festival, then he also went, not publicly but as it were in secret . . . . About the middle of the festival Jesus went up into the temple and began to teach (7:2–10, 14).

Let's begin with the occasion for going south from Galilee to the territory of Judea in which sits the Holy City of Jerusalem, and inside the city the magnificent temple built by King Herod the First. The Festival of Booths (Heb. *sukkōt*, otherwise known as the Feast of Tabernacles) was very popular during the period of the Second Temple. It was a weeklong festival that celebrated the ingathering of the crops from the land of promise. Its celebration was enjoined by the Lord in Exod 34:22. By this account it was an agricultural celebration that occurred in September/October. But the weeklong festival is described also in Leviticus where it is a celebration of liberation from slavery in Egypt, as follows: "You shall live in booths for seven days; all that are citizens in Israel shall live in booths, so that your generations may know that I made the people of Israel live in booths when I brought them out of the land of Egypt: I am the Lord your God" (Lev 23:42–43).

Whatever the festival celebrated, fruit of the land or freedom from slavery, it was a joyous time. Jewish pilgrims like the brothers of Jesus would pitch temporary shelters on the Mount of Olives overlooking the temple. They would eat their bread and drink their wine on the hillside with their relatives and friends. On the last great day of the festival (7:37), the high priest would go down to the Pool of Siloam with a golden pitcher to fetch fresh spring water. With his pitcher full of water he marched in procession up to the altar in the temple. On one side of the altar he poured the consecrated water, and on the other consecrated wine. Both elements flowed down into the cracks in the rock beneath, and thus enriched the whole earth. So the myth affirms. A full description of the significance of the Festival of Booths in Judaism can be found in the tractate *Sukkōt* in the Mishnah, the first significant work in rabbinic literature after the destruction of the temple in 70 CE.

No wonder the brothers want to go to such a festive celebration of life from the land, along with a measure of freedom from bondage. It would be a time to meet with relatives, friends, and neighbors. And no wonder the brothers want their older brother Jesus to join them in their journey south to such a celebration. They want him to use the occasion to demonstrate his power, evidenced in transforming water to wine, in healing a lame man at the pool of Beth-zatha, in feeding five thousand people from a few loaves and fish. It's puzzling to me how some scholars view the brothers' invitation for Jesus to join them on their journey to the festival as a sarcastic ploy to defame him in Judea. Well, maybe it should not be puzzling, given the parenthetical comment from the narrator: "(For not even his brothers believed in him)." The Merriam-Webster dictionary defines a parenthesis as "a remark or passage that departs from the theme of a discourse." That is the case here. The statement in parenthesis does not follow logically from the brothers' urging Jesus to go to the Festival of Booths with them.

A number of interpreters put much stock in the narrator's parenthetical remark, which then defames every other positive sign of a wholesome relationship between Jesus and his brothers. I'm glad the translators of the New Revised Standard Version put the offhand remark in brackets. That feature in a literary discussion usually means the reader could skip it and not miss anything important. I think that holds here, as I will explain shortly. The intrusiveness of the remark prompts this reader to view the bracketed statement as an interpolation by a later Christian scribe in the process of copying an earlier scroll. That copy was ultimately accepted into the New Testament canon as we have it. The effect of the bracketed statement is to have the reader think ill of the brothers of Jesus. Unfortunately, we do not have the original manuscript of the Fourth Gospel against which to test this scenario of mine. So brackets must suffice.

Complication continues. After Jesus declined the invitation of his brothers to join them in going to this particular festival, saying, "My time has not yet come," he is said to have remained in Galilee. But not for long apparently, because "after his brothers had gone to the festival, then he also went" (7:10). This peculiar course raises all kinds of questions. Did Jesus not like to travel with his brothers for some reason? Did he want to draw attention to himself by arriving later to the festival? Was he protecting his brothers from attack in the event of an uprising against his teaching in Jerusalem? There are no final answers to these questions. The teaching and action of Jesus could be offensive to the ears of traditional Jewish worshipers, just as some Christian preachers today (including myself) offend some members of a congregation.

Let's say, for the sake of argument, the brothers did take some offense at their brother's far-out words and deeds. Many disciples did the same. Following the feeding of the multitude many took offense. Jesus said he was the living bread that came down from heaven, echoing the gift of special manna in the desert to sustain the Hebrews. "When many of his disciples heard it, they said, 'This teaching is difficult; who can accept it?' . . . Because of this many of his disciples turned back and no longer went about with him" (6:60, 66). In their time and place and situation the words and actions of Jesus were doubtless offensive to contemporary Jewish minds. His critical demonstration in the temple court, for example, was bound to offend the priestly leaders especially (2:13–25). The same is true for some present-day Christian communities when a leader challenges a point of doctrine or practice. I have known modern congregations to divide when some members called for equal opportunity for women and men to be ordained for pastoral leadership in congregations.

A Complicated Love Story

There is one more riddle in this text that challenges reason. When Jesus did decide to go to Jerusalem for the Festival of Booths after his brothers had gone, it is said that he went "not publicly but as it were in secret" (7:10). But the secret, whatever form it took, did not remain a secret in Jerusalem. Our narrator addresses this matter thus: "About the middle of the festival Jesus went up into the temple and began to teach. The Jews were astonished at it, saying, 'How does this man have such learning, when he has never been taught?'" (7:14–15). No place is more open and more crowded than the temple precincts on a high holiday. It was a place for people to talk, for priests and scribes to teach and worship. It was not unusual for someone endowed with communication skills to speak in an open court of the temple. Jesus had such skills, according to "the Jews" who heard him. I shall probe this troubling group title, "the Jews," in a later chapter. Meanwhile, a brief comment would be in order. "The Jews" in the Fourth Gospel is *not* an all-encompassing term referring to all Jewish people of every status and place and time. The negative edge of the label in the voice of Jesus in this Gospel can result in caustic "anti-Semitism," with tragic consequences in some cases. Keep in mind Jesus was thoroughly Jewish, as were his parents, brothers, and disciples all. Hence their glad participation in the festive celebrations in Jerusalem.

POST-RESURRECTION ANNOUNCEMENT SENT TO "MY BROTHERS"

Jesus had a good relationship with Mary Magdalene, and she with him. Her grief at his crucifixion comes through in chapter 20. When she came to the new tomb in which Nicodemus and Joseph of Arimathea had expeditiously placed the body of Jesus out of respect for the Day of Preparation and the Sabbath, she found the tomb empty. Then the risen Jesus greeted her thus:

> Jesus said to her, "Mary!" She turned and said to him in Hebrew, "Rabbouni!" (which means Teacher). Jesus said to her, "Do not hold on to me, because I have not yet ascended to the Father. But go to my brothers and say to them, 'I am ascending to my Father and your Father, to my God and your God.'" Mary Magdalene went and announced to the disciples, "I have seen the Lord"; and she told them that he had said these things to her. (20:16–18)

You can see the problem here. Mary's mission from Jesus was to "go to my brothers" with an astonishing announcement about his upcoming ascension to Father God. But Mary, it would seem, decided to go instead to the disciples with the word from the risen Jesus. Questions come to mind in a flash. Why would Mary go to the disciples when she was told to go to the brothers of Jesus? Were "my brothers" part of the group of disciples, and thus implicitly included? I think the last question calls for an answer of "yes."

The brothers of Jesus believed in his mission. They accompanied him to Jerusalem for the observance of Passover, and remained in that city after his death. Some commentators think otherwise. They claim that "brothers" implies disciples, not biological brothers. So the notion is that "my brothers" in this text implies "my disciples." I find that idea far-fetched. "Disciples" is a more inclusive term than "brothers." So why use the more restrictive word? We know that the brothers of Jesus along with their mother were in Jerusalem during and after the crucifixion. And they really did believe in his word and his work, as the next section will prove beyond the shadow of a doubt.

THE PEOPLE IN AN UPSTAIRS ROOM FOLLOWING THE CRUCIFIXION-RESURRECTION

The book of Acts was probably written a short time before the Fourth Gospel. The first chapter of that book identifies a group of faithful followers of Jesus gathered in an upstairs room in the aftermath of his death, and the joy of his resurrection. Here is the list.

> Then they returned to Jerusalem from the mount called Olivet, which is near Jerusalem, a sabbath day's journey away. When they had entered the city, they went to the room upstairs where they were staying, Peter, and John, and James and Andrew, Philip and Thomas, Bartholomew and Matthew, James son of Alphaeus, and Simon the Zealot, and Judas son of James. All these were constantly devoting themselves to prayer, together with certain women, including Mary the mother of Jesus, *as well as his brothers* (Acts 1:12–14).

A few observations are in order. The group remained in Jerusalem following Jesus's death and resurrection, because Jesus had instructed them to do so while they wait for the promised Holy Spirit. They found an upstairs room where they would all meet and wait. Oddly enough, the author of Acts felt constrained to give the name of every disciple, then added the name "Mary the mother of Jesus," and finally includes, as a kind of forced entry, "as well as his brothers." There is something about the brothers of Jesus that stifles the author of Luke and Acts from giving the brothers of Jesus any significant recognition in their faithful support of Jesus. But there they are in any case in the upstairs room awaiting the descent of the Spirit.

The author of Acts, attempting to give a worthy account of the development of the earliest community of Jesus, cannot escape the significance of one brother in particular, namely, James. This James is unidentified in Acts apart from his very common Jewish name (literally, "Jacob"), even though he became the chief leader of the Jerusalem community of Christ-followers. This James is none other than the brother of Jesus, the second oldest of the family. He is the one who gives the final word on a sticky issue having to do with Paul's efforts to advance the mission to the gentiles (see Acts 15). It is mysterious why the significant identity of this James—among so many others with the same name—is missing from Acts. He was the faithful brother of Jesus. After Jesus's departure from the world James served the community in Jerusalem faithfully in the name of his older brother until about 62 CE. He was killed by a rogue high priest of the time, who was then banished by the incoming Roman prefect. But there's more.

Acts was written long after Paul's mission and letter-writing in the fifties. Paul knew James the brother of Jesus personally, as well as the other brothers of Jesus. The author of Acts probably did not. So now we need to check on the early testimony of Paul in his letters written some time between 49 and 56 CE.

Paul speaks of three metaphorical "pillars" on which the emerging community of Jesus rests. They are James, Peter, and John, in that order (Gal 2:9). This James, standing in first place in Paul's list of three, is none other than the biological brother of Jesus. We know that, because Paul tells us so. He actually met this brother of Jesus during one of his visits to Jerusalem, and identifies him explicitly. "After three years I did go up to Jerusalem to visit Cephas [Peter] and stayed with him fifteen days; but I did not see any other apostle except James the Lord's brother" (Gal 1:18–19). The Lord Jesus, that is. Paul in Galatians—unlike the author of Acts—has no hesitation in giving clear identity to the brother next in age to Jesus. James and Paul were living and working in the same mission at the same time: James the brother of Jesus in Jerusalem and Paul elsewhere in the north Mediterranean territory.

But there's more. Paul affirms that the risen Jesus appeared to James, and that ahead of all the apostles: "Then he appeared to James, then to all the apostles" (1 Cor 15:7). This is the same James that Paul identified in Galatians as "brother of the Lord" Jesus.

But what of the other brothers described parenthetically in the Fourth Gospel as not believing in their brother Jesus (7:5)? Again, Paul lets us know, ever so briefly but assuredly, what they did in the Spirit of the risen Jesus, their brother. The context of the brief reference should be cited. Paul had trouble with some critics in the Christ community in the city of Corinth. Some of them thought Paul was in mission in the name of Jesus Christ to secure money for himself. He counters their charge with several rhetorical questions, within which we find a reference to the brothers of Jesus who work in mission and receive a reward for doing so. "This is my defense," says Paul, "to those who would examine me. Do we not have the right to our food and drink? Do we not have the right to be accompanied by a believing wife, as do the other apostles and *the brothers of the Lord* and Cephas?" (1 Cor 9:3–5) So the brothers of the Lord, the ones we found in the room upstairs in Jerusalem, were busy in post-resurrection mission alongside the apostles of Jesus.

This calls into serious question the bracketed comment in the Fourth Gospel at 7:5: "(For not even his brothers believed in him)." In whatever manner Jesus was conceived in his mother's womb, he had biological brothers born of Mary. They lived together for about twenty-five years in the little village of Nazareth in Galilee, attended the same Jewish synagogue, and ate at the same table. By the time Jesus launched his mission in Galilee, his father, Joseph, had passed away. The words and actions of Jesus pushed the boundaries of the long-established religion of Judaism. His mother and his brothers might well have disowned him for pushing those boundaries to the extent that he did. But they did not disown him. His brother, James, donned the mantle that Jesus left behind and worked faithfully to extend "the kingdom of God" centered in Jerusalem.

7

Signs of a Super Physician

GOOD HEALTH AND LONG life together constitute a deep desire rooted in the human psyche. But the same human family knows only too well that the flesh in which we all live is subject to the ravages of time, disease, and death. It seems unfair to inherit the desire to live forever, knowing from experience that the precious life span on earth has a limit. So the human urge is to conceive another reality beyond flesh that perishes. Where and how that other reality exists is forever mystery. Of course, we can imagine it, read about it, and propose a realm of consciousness flesh-free. And we humans do all of that using the same fleshly parameters with which we are familiar. One could spin this scenario in many directions, and for a long time. But we would be obliged to come back to the starting point of human imagination that longs to be free of the flesh that perishes, and still have thoughtful, meaningful, endless life somewhere, somehow.

We come now to the three "signs" of healing—labeled thus exclusively in the Fourth Gospel—in an attempt to grasp their significance in relation to the human urge to live forever free from the grip of disease, age, and death. These three "signs" do not include the resuscitation of Jesus's friend, Lazarus. That episode is still "sign," albeit of immense proportion compared to the three healings preceding it. Those three human subjects were still breathing when the healing happened. Lazarus was not. So the resuscitation of Lazarus caps the three healing signs preceding. I have reserved a separate, short chapter following this one to highlight some key features of the Lazarus episode.

SIGNS OF A SUPER PHYSICIAN

HEALING AN OFFICIAL'S SON FROM A DISTANCE (4:46–54)

Jesus is in Galilee, familiar territory for him. A man of some importance came to him in what appears to be a state of desperation. The man is said to be a "royal official" whose little son had fallen ill to the point of death. The official must have heard something about the power of Jesus to heal, even though there is no record in the Fourth Gospel of Jesus healing anyone to that point. There was the "sign" of changing water to wine at Cana. The royal official may have heard about the creative work had done in Galilee, and appealed to him to change the sad condition of Jesus, as he had changed the sad condition at the wedding in Cana.

The stated identity of this father is at best veiled. The NRSV uses the term "royal official." What might that term signify in Galilee? King Herod Antipas was the recognized head of the region at the time of Jesus's ministry. Presumably, he would qualify for the title, "royal official." But it is unlikely "that fox" (Luke 11:32) would seek out Jesus for any good reason. The father of the boy may have been a courtier of some sort in Herod's household: in that sense "royal official." Or Herod Antipas may have appointed him head of the town of Capernaum in the order of a mayor. The clues within the title require additional information to become more than a guess. At any rate, the distraught official approaches Jesus with some implied knowledge of his unusual power. Jesus simply tells the official that his son will live, with no attempt made on the part of Jesus to go to the son and lay hands on him. The royal official has to trust the word of Jesus without reservation. That kind of trust becomes increasingly a major theme in the Fourth Gospel.

The royal official soon learns from his slaves that his son is alive and well. There is no recorded attempt on the part of the official to seek out Jesus to offer a word of gratitude. He simply goes on his way believing in the healing word of Jesus: "Go; your son will live" (4:50).

This is the shortest and least significant of the three healing signs. The next two in turn illustrate increased intensity, each one moving forward into the all-encompassing "sign" of life beyond mortality, accomplished singularly through the death and resurrection of Jesus himself.

A Complicated Love Story

HEALING A LONG-TIME CRIPPLE AT THE POOL OF BETH-ZATHA IN JERUSALEM (5:1–9)

The intention of the discussion in this book is to grapple with the shape and substance of the literature as it stands in the Fourth Gospel. Once in a while it will be tempting to engage the material at another level. Nowhere is that temptation greater than in chapter 5. Here are some questions that spring to mind immediately. Was there such a pool of water at the time of Jesus? Does archaeology support the description in the Fourth Gospel? What gave this pool its extraordinary capacity to heal? Is there some significance to the number of colonnades? A brief response to these questions must suffice for our purposes. At least one of them must remain unanswered: what gave the pool its healing power?

In the nineteenth century a group of archaeologists discovered the remains of such a pool located in the Muslim Quarter of Jerusalem. It appears that a waterfall had created a depression in the rock below that held the bubbling water. The five colonnades surrounding the pool were places where invalids waited for the bubbling effect of the water, believed to promote healing.

The number five becomes important symbolically in the Fourth Gospel. The five scrolls of Israel's Law were believed to be the revelation of God's will for the people of Israel. The stories and directives in the five scrolls were binding for the people that God had brought into being out of bondage. As one might expect, the number five is significant in the Fourth Gospel, anchored as that Gospel is in the tradition of ancient Israel: the Samaritan woman had *five* husbands (4:18); the pool of Beth-zatha in Jerusalem had *five* porticoes (5:2); a boy had *five* barley loaves that Jesus used to feed a multitude (6:9); the number of people fed were *five* thousand (6:10). It is not surprising, then, that there were precisely *twelve* baskets of fragments gathered after the meal by the *twelve* disciples (6:12–13), reminiscent of the *twelve tribes* that constituted ancient Israel to whom God gave the five scrolls of the Law. Obeying the directives in the five scrolls of the Torah/Law created a distinct identity for the people of Israel. Sabbath observance in particular was an important commandment of the Law that marked the Jewish people off from their non-Jewish neighbors.

Time now to peer inside the story about Jesus in relation to one crippled man in particular lying beside the pool of bubbling water.

Apparently the man had a hard time getting into the pool when the water was believed to transmit its healing power. This man had been ill for thirty-eight years. Hard to imagine! He must have had patience galore. Other sick people at the pool apparently had the ability to get into the water at the right time. This one man did not. Jesus's question to him seems out of place: "Do you want to be made well?" (5:6). Of course he does, except that the more mobile comrades crowd him out when the healing moment strikes. I've tried to grasp the situation, but without much success: a man waiting at the edge of the life-giving pool day after day for the healing waters, but without success. The five-porch people seem to have been self-serving. No one made an effort to put this man into the water at the auspicious time. Then Jesus comes along. But he does not put the crippled man into the pool either, as if to call into question the proffered healing power of the pool, or the indifference of the people to the man. Instead, Jesus heals him using his own power-packed *word* quite apart from the proffered power of the pool: "Stand up, take your mat and walk." The man obeyed the word of Jesus and walked away carrying his mat after being thirty-eight years a cripple (5:8).

Then the story takes another turn. The day on which the healing happened was not like every other day of the week in Jerusalem. It was the Sabbath day. Remember the five scrolls that Israel's God generated for the elect people of Israel? Devout Jewish people at the time of Jesus sought to keep faith with their heritage, especially in relation to those five scrolls. One of the distinctive rules of that Law was proper Sabbath observance. Devout Jewish people committed themselves to keeping Sabbath in honor of their God who gave the Sabbath Law to be obeyed.

Now here's the rub. Jesus healed the man on the Sabbath, and ordered him to take up his mat and walk on the Sabbath. Both actions would have constituted work. Sabbath in Jewish Law means *rest from all work* performed on the other days of the week: "Remember the sabbath day, and keep it holy. Six days you shall labor and do all your work. But the seventh day is a sabbath to the LORD your God; you shall not do any work—you, your son or your daughter, your male or female slave, your livestock, or the alien resident in your towns" (Exod 20:8–10; Deut 5:12–14).

Observance of this rule of Jewish Law, among others, identified the Jewish people as belonging to their God, *Yahweh*. Apparently, Jesus considered the act of healing the invalid man, and the act of his carrying a mat, as life-giving acts that trumped the Law of Sabbath. Again, Jewish identity was at stake. Proper Sabbath keeping was not merely a good idea hatched in the minds of the Jewish people of Jesus's time. Nor was it a burden to keep the Sabbath. On the contrary, the Jewish teachers delighted in the Law of the Lord that distinguished them from their non-Jewish neighbors. For the teachers especially, the Law represented the will of God for his people. Yet Jesus boldly challenged the Sabbath mark of identity when it came into conflict with granting newness of life to a man crippled for some thirty-eight years. Even so, a Jewish observer might ask: Could the healing and the walking with the mat not wait one more day? The man had been waiting thirty-eight years to be healed.

The Jewish leaders also had difficulty with the way Jesus identified himself, "calling God his own Father, thereby making himself equal to God" (5:18). I think I understand their problem. If I had been there at that time as a devout Jewish observer, and heard the claim of Jesus as it appears in the Fourth Gospel, I probably would have thought and felt the same. Beyond that, I have some difficulty with the statement Jesus made to the healed man when the two men met up later. Here it is: "See, you have been made well! Do not sin any more, so that nothing worse happens to you" (5:15). This comment raises troubling questions for me. Was the man's long illness because of some sin he had committed? Are sin and suffering somehow intertwined? Let's just say, if I were visiting a sick person in hospital in our world, as I have done many times, I could not bring myself to say such a thing to the person lying in a hospital bed. I have visited with some of the most faithful people of God afflicted with dreadful diseases. I would not dare attribute their diseases to some sin in their lives. The obvious fact of human life on earth is that the righteous and the sinner alike are subject to the same aging process, the same afflictions, and die from one or another of the same diseases.

Granted, some people act irresponsibly in ways that lead to illness. Some overeat, while others smoke tobacco. Some are careless on a building site, while others swim out too far into the ocean. All of these are irresponsible acts or habits. But I doubt that these examples measure up to the warning Jesus gives to the onetime cripple at 5:15: "Do not sin any more, so that nothing worse happens to you." We simply do not know what specific sin might be implied. Ironically, breaking the Sabbath command would be considered a sin in ancient Israel and in first-century Judaism.

And one more point: by the end of the first century CE, leaders in the new Christian movement had changed the day of Sabbath rest from the seventh to the first day of the week in light of the resurrection of Jesus on the first day. The author of the Fourth Gospel was doubtless well-aware of the change to the first day, and highlights the tension between the traditional

Jewish way of observing Sabbath on the seventh day and the new, less strict, Christian way of keeping Sabbath on the first day. Furthermore, following Paul's gentile world mission (ca. 50–60 CE), non-Jewish males in the Christian congregations were not required to be circumcised, or to eat kosher food, or keep Sabbath on the seventh day, all of these being important regulations for the Jewish people. The Sabbath controversies in the Fourth Gospel echo such points of tension between the renewed Judaism (post-70 CE) on the one hand, and the new Christianity at the turn of the second century on the other. It is highly doubtful that Jesus made any attempt to change the day of the week for observing Sabbath, or for the way of keeping that day holy unto the Lord, *Yahweh*.

HEALING A MAN BORN BLIND (9:1–41)

Notice the increasing intensity of the problem in each of the three healings. The official's young son had fallen ill and might die. Jesus healed him from a distance. Then the lame man had suffered his condition for thirty-eight years when Jesus healed him. And now in chapter 9 the blind man had been blind from birth when Jesus healed him. Imagine the feeling of a person blind from birth: unable to see a full moon, the color of daffodils, of peas and cauliflower on the plate, and so much more.

Here's the point. The increase in the intensity of each illness, together with the ascending degrees of joy that must have accrued from the newness of life in each case, all point *beyond* these three signs. If we follow the pattern we come across dead Lazarus whom Jesus resuscitated after being dead four days. But even that astounding feat is not the climax of the newness of life in the Fourth Gospel. The resurrected state of Jesus after three days in a tomb is the climax. That extraordinary newness of life is then extended from Jesus to those who identify fully and faithfully with him. They too are said to receive the same newness of life that ultimately transcends sickness and death to which all flesh is heir.

Again, we bump up against the matter of sin in relation to illness. This time it comes from the disciples of Jesus: "Rabbi, who sinned, this man or his parents, that he was born blind?" (9:2). On the surface, their question is just silly. How could the unborn infant commit sin and thus be born blind? And to suggest that the ill effect of the parents' sin was passed along mysteriously to the genetic makeup of the infant is equally infantile. Jesus's answer dispels such wrongheaded thinking. In this case, says Jesus, "he was born blind so that God's works might be revealed in him" (9:3). Here we have from Jesus a positive element embedded in an otherwise negative state of blindness.

Jesus then declares auspiciously, "I am the light of the world" (9:5). This is one of many times Jesus utters the "I am" sayings about his reason for being in the world of sin, disease, disaster, and death. Even though the phrase "I am" can be found in the voice of Jesus in the Synoptic Gospels, it comes through in a powerfully existential mode in the Fourth Gospel. Here is a classic example: "Very truly, I tell you, before Abraham was, *I am*" (8:58; cf. 6:35–51; 10:9, 11; 11:25; 14:6, 20; 15:1–5; 18:5–6).

We come now to the unconventional way in which Jesus healed the blind man. "Jesus spat on the ground and made mud with his saliva and spread the mud on the man's eyes" (9:6). As noted already, water imagery is plentiful in the Fourth Gospel: water is the universal element in giving and sustaining life on earth. But this kind of saliva-water comes directly from the personal inner being of the life-giving Jesus. The man is then told to go to the renowned water supply in the pool of Siloam, to wash off the mud, and thus receive his sight (9:7).

The water of Siloam had a long history dating back to the reign of King Hezekiah (715–686 BCE). He commissioned two groups of workers to excavate through rock, one group starting from inside Jerusalem and the other from outside the city wall in the Kidron valley where the Gihon spring was located. The two groups met in the middle on the same level, and the water flowed. That remarkable feat meant that an enemy could not cut off the water supply from the inhabitants of the city of David. In no small measure, the Siloam water became a source of life for Jewish people of Jerusalem, particularly during the Second Temple period. The blind man used that same historic water flow to wash the mud from his eyes. And behold he was able to see for the first time in his life. One can only imagine the man's exhilaration in seeing his world for the first time. He appears to have handled the experience with ease. Then come the questions from the various observers.

The *neighbors* see him and recognize him as the man born blind. Some think he is like him, but not really the man. The now-sighted man insists, "I am the man" (9:9). Rather than praising the Lord for such a marvelous benefit for their once-blind neighbor, they were skeptical. They brought the man to the learned *Pharisees* for a more sophisticated answer. Note, the act of healing happened on the Sabbath. "Some of the Pharisees said, 'This man is not from God, for he does not observe the sabbath'" (9:16). After questioning the man about the identity of the one who healed him, they approached the man's *parents*. They sidestepped the question thus: "We know that this is our son, and that he was born blind; but we do not know how it is that now he sees, nor do we know who opened his eyes. Ask him; he is of age. He will speak for himself" (9:20–21). They value their place within their Jewish tradition and worship, and they know the power of their educated leaders.

Their rather guarded answer, according to the narrator, was because they did not want to be put out of the synagogue. There you have it. "The Jews had already agreed that anyone who confessed Jesus to be the Messiah would be put out of the synagogue. Therefore his parents said, 'He is of age; ask him'" (9:23). This exclusion from synagogue worship was exactly what happened to the Jewish Christian group to whom this Fourth Gospel was directed at the turn of the second century. They had hailed the risen Jesus as Messiah, and found themselves thereby excluded from the traditional Jewish way of worship in the synagogue.

Sometime between 85 CE and 115 CE, the Jewish rabbis at Jamnia, under the leadership of Rabbi Gamaliel, drafted a *Benediction Against Heretics*. It was directed particularly against Jewish converts to the new community of Jesus Messiah.[5] The converts still read the same Jewish Scriptures, but added a powerful messianic factor in the person of risen Jesus, which tended to diminish the stature of Moses and the Law. The latter was the heart of Jewish life and thought, as it is to this day. These measures coming out of Jamnia corresponded with the formation and development of the Messianic community to which the Fourth Gospel was directed. Loud echoes of the *Benediction Against Heretics* come through especially in chapter 9, where the once-blind man was put out of the synagogue, and his parents were afraid of being put out (9:22). The same fear of excommunication from the synagogue comes through also in chapter 12, where "many, even of the authorities, believed in him. But because of the Pharisees they did not confess it, for fear that they would be put out of the synagogue" (12:42). "The Pharisees" in this context identify leading Jews devoted to a right interpretation of the Law, on the one hand, and a declaration of excommunication of heretics from the Jewish worship on the other.

As a result, some Jewish converts to Jesus Messiah abandoned their Christian confession, and were thereby able to return to synagogue worship and teaching. The number of *Jewish* Christ-followers in the new community

---

5. Martyn, *History and Theology*, 46–66.

of Messiah dwindled during the second and third centuries until the community of the *Jewish* Jesus became more and more gentile. Moreover, the comment about the expelling of the once-blind man, and that of the man's parents, reflects what actually happened around the time when this Gospel was written.

The man, now seeing, continued to defend Jesus boldly against the educated Pharisees who could not believe that Jesus came from God. "Here is an astonishing thing!" said the enlightened man, "You do not know where he comes from, and yet he opened my eyes. We know that God does not listen to sinners, but he does listen to one who worships him and obeys his will. Never since the world began has it been heard that anyone opened the eyes of a person born blind. If this man were not from God, he could do nothing" (9:30–33). What a testimonial! What bold bravery! But the learned Pharisees could not get past their tradition, and the healed man suffered. "They answered him, 'You were born entirely in sins, and are you trying to teach us?' And they drove him out" (9.34). Here we now have the view of the Pharisees on the relationship of sin to disease. They too assume some link between human suffering and sin, as in the victim violating the good law of God.

Jesus returns to the man now excluded from the synagogue, and reveals himself as the Son of Man. The man, now seeing as the Pharisees did not, responds: "Lord I believe" (9:38). Simple yet profound.

8

Lazarus of Bethany

BETHLEHEM IS MUCH MORE famous than Bethany, thanks to the opening chapters of Matthew and Luke where Bethlehem is cited as the birthplace of Jesus. Beyond those opening chapters of Matthew and Luke the town of Bethlehem is mentioned elsewhere only once in the New Testament, and that in the Fourth Gospel in an argument between some Judeans (7:42). Nor is there any record of Jesus ever visiting Bethlehem. But he did visit the town of Bethany. He had three beloved friends living there, Mary, Martha, and Lazarus. It was also in Bethany that Jesus stayed in the home of Simon the Leper, the house where a woman anointed Jesus with expensive ointment (Matt 26:6; Mark 14:3). Bethany was located about 1.5 miles east of Jerusalem on the southeastern slope of the Mount of Olives. The remains of a house at the site dates back about two thousand years, and is believed to represent the house of the three siblings in our story. Solid evidence to this effect is not available. A tomb was also found near the house, said to be the tomb of Lazarus. The text in focus is 11:1–44.

The meaning of the name Bethany has been debated. The first part of the word is straightforward. "Beth" is Hebrew for "house." The second part is debatable. One scholar from the nineteenth century suggested "House of Dates." That has since been challenged. A more likely reading is "House of Misery," or "Poor House." The inhabitants allowed Simon the Leper to live among them, presumably because the townspeople in Bethany welcomed the sick and infirm to live among them without recrimination. As noted already, Jesus chose to stay in the home of Simon the Leper.

Perhaps the best way to capture the many-sided story surrounding the resuscitation of Lazarus by the word of Jesus would be to set out headings under which to discuss the various short episodes.

A Complicated Love Story

LOVE ABOUNDING

The strong theme of love in the Fourth Gospel comes to full flower in the second part of the Gospel, beginning with the moving story in which Jesus brings his beloved friend, Lazarus, back to life. Love abounds throughout the episode. But before we take up that theme I should explain why I call the action of Jesus on the deceased Lazarus resuscitation rather than resurrection.

If the resurrection of Jesus after his death by crucifixion was *not* a return to mortal flesh and blood, but to a transcendent form of being, no longer subject to death, then we should not use the term "resurrection" to describe the return of Lazarus to his mortal life. The resurrected Jesus could appear in a room with the doors locked, and disappear without opening a door (20:19, 26). However we may explain the empty tomb that belonged to someone other than Jesus's family, it surely must not mean the return of Jesus to the flesh-and-blood experience of mortals. Jesus died once for all, and was raised into a new and different realm of existence. I appeal to the insight of the apostle Paul in support of this position: "flesh and blood cannot inherit the kingdom of God, nor does the perishable inherit the imperishable" (1 Cor 15:50). There is no indication that Lazarus was given an imperishable body when Jesus called him to come out of the tomb. Lazarus was brought back to the life he had before he died, only to die again later. The resurrected Jesus did not die again. I think we have to admit such resurrected existence is wrapped in mystery, however much we may sing the Easter hymns and shout in unison on Easter Sunday morning, "He is risen. He is risen indeed." Do we really mean Jesus came back to the same *mortal* life he had when he was tried and crucified? I should think not.

Returning now to the story of love that so energized Jesus to give hope and comfort to his two women friends, Mary and Martha, who had lost their brother, Lazarus. Jesus was not in the vicinity of Bethany when Lazarus fell ill. He wasn't even in Judea (11:7). Yet somehow the two sisters were able to send a message to Jesus: "Lord, he whom you love is ill" (11:3). Here is one of the peculiar features in the Fourth Gospel: Jesus is said to love particular individuals. As far as we know, Lazarus was not one of the disciples of Jesus. We know from this Fourth Gospel about one *unnamed* disciple whom Jesus loved, and the other disciples seemed to know as much without taking offence. Some scholars suggest Lazarus was that beloved disciple. But without more solid evidence the case is still open. More on the beloved disciple later.

Of course, when Mary and Martha say that Jesus loved their brother, it does not mean exclusively. He loved others too in a special way, no doubt, including Mary and Martha themselves: "Jesus loved Martha and her sister and Lazarus" (11:5). It just seems strange to read that Jesus loved particular people within his circle of friends and disciples. Perhaps the same is true of all of us in some measure. We are drawn to some personalities more than others. What I find interesting in this part of the story is that some "Jews" who knew Lazarus, and who came alongside Mary and Martha to mourn his passing, remark on this love-relationship Jesus had with Lazarus. They say: "See how he [Jesus] loved him!" (11:36).

DELIBERATE DELAY

When Martha's message about her brother's illness reached Jesus, he responded in a most peculiar way. His disciples urged him to be on his way to Bethany posthaste. But he lingered in the same place, far from Bethany, in the assurance that "this illness does not lead to death" (11:4). With that thought in mind, Jesus "stayed two days longer in the place where he was" (11:6). The rationale for staying two days longer is not clear, except that Jesus had said that the illness would not lead to death. What he meant by that statement is difficult to fathom in light of the ensuing events. He told his disciples, "Our friend Lazarus has fallen asleep, but I am going there to awaken him" (11:11). Meanwhile, Mary and Martha had their brother's lifeless body placed in a tomb. Then Jesus tells his puzzled disciples plainly, "Lazarus is dead . . . let us go to him" (11:14–15).

By the time Jesus reached Bethany, Lazarus had been dead four days. How that squares with Jesus's comment to his followers that the illness would *not* lead to death is difficult to grasp. If the delay was meant to test the faith of his friends and disciples, it certainly did that. What, then, are we to make of Jesus's prediction?

It may be argued that Jesus's two-day delay in reaching Bethany was to make the miracle more dramatic to convince the people watching that he had access to the power of God that conquers death. Death is assumed to be the enemy of humanity. Every healthy human being wants to avoid death at all costs. It's built into the human psyche. But disease, aging, and dying are linked and inevitable, like it or not. Jesus's delay in reaching Lazarus may serve to prove that there is a power greater than mortality: a power of life. Lazarus is not given voice on the matter. No one questions him, however tempting it may have been to do so. The story does not allow it. Not even a word of thanks from Lazarus to Jesus. Someone might have wanted to ask him how it feels to be restored to his old life again. But no one asks anything of Lazarus. And he says nothing.

LOGIC AND FAITH

By the time Jesus reached Bethany, "Lazarus had already been in the tomb four days" (11:17). Martha knew the law of decomposition. She also believed that if Jesus had been in Bethany her brother would not have died. She was working with everyday logic, coupled with a good measure of faith in the power of Jesus. Ponder the dialogue between her and Jesus: "Lord, if you had been here, my brother would not have died. But even now I know that God will give you whatever you ask of him" (11:32). Her first sentence comes out of experience. She knew that Jesus had healed others. She knew also that Jesus loved Lazarus, and would use his life-giving power to heal him as he had done for others. People who are still alive can be healed. We've had that in the Fourth Gospel up to this point. But Martha goes beyond her mixture of logic and faith. It takes a bit of coaxing to do so.

Jesus announces, "Your brother will rise again" (11:23). Then Martha brings her Jewish knowledge of end-time resurrection to the fore, and knows her brother will participate in that. But Jesus introduces something far more puzzling, not anything like the doctrine of end-time resurrection. He says: "*I am* the resurrection and the life. Those who believe in me, even though they die, will live, and everyone who lives and believes in me will never die" (11:25–26). Here is a classic case of the "I am" sayings in the Fourth Gospel. Jesus does not point to a future event of immense proportion, but to immortal life lived in the present by faith in Jesus. But Jesus goes even beyond that: "Everyone who lives and believes in me will never die" (11:26). I cannot speak for others, but I find this cryptic message of Jesus scarcely comprehensible. Either my logic is faulty, or my faith is weak.

Here is my best guess. Solid faith in the life, and grace, and power of Jesus will mean that death is merely a transition out of mortality into immortality. But that logic does not quite square with the terms of the text: "Everyone who lives and believes in me will never die." Jesus in this Gospel asks his audience in Bethany, particularly Martha, "Do you believe this?" (11:26). Her answer does not speak directly to what Jesus said. She may have had as much difficulty with Jesus's declaration as I do. "She said to him, 'Yes, Lord, I believe that you are the Messiah, the Son of God, the one coming into the world'" (11:27). I could go along with that. But it does not speak to the declaration of Jesus as it stands, or to his question following: "Everyone who lives and believes in me will never die. Do you believe this?" I have watched faithful people of profound faith in Jesus Christ go through the harrowing process of dying. It was heart-wrenching.

MEANING OF TEARS

Water is very present and powerful within the Fourth Gospel. Water, like the air we breathe, gives and sustains human and animal and plant life. One might think the episode about Lazarus is devoid of any water imagery. Not so. Water is present in the tears of the various participants at the tomb, including the tears of Jesus.

> When Mary came where Jesus was and saw him, she knelt at his feet and said to him, "Lord, if you had been here, my brother would not have died." When Jesus saw her *weeping*, and the Jews who came with her also *weeping*, he was greatly disturbed in spirit and deeply moved. He said, "Where have you laid him?" They said to him, "Lord, come and see." Jesus began to *weep*. (11:32–35)

Tears can signal more than one emotion. Often they mean disappointment, sadness, and loss. But they can also mean tears of joy. Both Mary's weeping and that of the Jews who were with her seem to signal a normal sense of loss at the death of a loved one. That would certainly be true of Mary. She had lost her beloved brother. The Jews present may have been overcome by Mary's weeping, and joined her uncontrollably. As for Jesus's weeping, I think his tears may have signaled sadness about the ravages of mortality that put his beloved Lazarus in the tomb. But more likely, the reader should see something different in the tears rolling down the cheeks of Jesus. In this respect it may be noted that the Greek word used for Jesus's "weeping" (*dakruō*) is different from the one depicting the tears of Mary and the Jews (*klaiō*). The difference may signal nothing more than alternate words for the same emotion, as we have also in English: "weep" and "cry." But I think there is more to the use of the two different terms in this story.

If I may apply this to the two terms for shedding tears in relation to Lazarus, I would say that Mary and the Jews with her were expressing appropriate emotional response to the loss of a loved one. It appears the term used for the tearful emotion of Jesus would be the stronger one of the two:

Jesus was really weeping deeply and noticeably. This is borne out by the narrator's comment: "he was greatly disturbed in spirit and deeply moved" (11:33). So his tears issued from deep emotional and—dare I say it—theological grief related to the painful loss of the earthly life of a beloved friend.

Yet there is another way to view the tearful expression of Jesus on this occasion. His tears could well be construed as tears of hope in eternal life, which he offers to all who put their trust in him. If an earthly life-span of X years is all there is to human existence, then I think we are driven to join in Peggy Lee's lament: "if that's all there is, then let's keep dancing . . . if that's all there is."

UNBOUND

Before making any comment on the last part of the story about Lazarus revived, it would be well to let the relevant text meet our minds on its own terms. However familiar the text may be, rereading it lets its every nuance register in our postmodern minds and hearts. Let the strangeness of the narrative have its way. This is not everyday language and action for us in our world. If you find some parts baffling, let it be so. You can come back again and again and find another flash of insight to help you on your path of faithfulness. Here is the script about Lazarus revived.

> Then Jesus, again greatly disturbed, came to the tomb. It was a cave, and a stone was lying against it. Jesus said, "Take away the stone." Martha, the sister of the dead man, said to him, "Lord, already there is a stench because he has been dead four days." Jesus said to her, "Did I not tell you that if you believed, you would see the glory of God?" So they took away the stone. And Jesus looked upward and said, "Father, I thank you for having heard me. I knew that you always hear me, but I have said this for the sake of the crowd standing here, so that they may believe that you sent me." When he had said this, he cried with a loud voice, *"Lazarus, come out!"* The dead man came out, his hands and feet bound with strips of cloth, and his face wrapped in a cloth. Jesus said to them, *"Unbind him, and let him go."* (11:38–44)

Jesus, standing near the tomb, gives an order in the presence of the crowd that had gathered (11:42). Why the *crowd* had gathered is not clear. A crowd in the little village of Bethany might number no more than twenty or thirty. This crowd had not gathered at this time for the burial of Lazarus. Martha's comment to Jesus confirms that Lazarus was entombed four days earlier. The crowd probably gathered to see what feat Jesus would perform among them. His reputation for healing and helping people would have drawn people to him.

When Jesus said, "Take away the stone," he must have been addressing the command to some people nearby, even though Martha's name follows the command. Martha would have had a hard time moving the stone by herself. Her response was not about the stone, but about the condition of Lazarus. Her brother had been dead four days. She was concerned about "the stench." Hers was a cultural response to an otherwise highly unusual command. Martha, like most of us still, was familiar with sociocultural mores. Some people took away the stone. And Jesus then prayed.

As noted previously regarding the long prayer of Jesus in chapter 17, so also the shorter prayer here in chapter 11. How did the author of the Fourth Gospel know the prayer of Jesus word for word? He would have been writing some seventy years after the time of Jesus. It may be that the disciples paid close attention to the wording of the prayers of Jesus, even a spontaneous prayer such as this one. I think it is likely that the author of this Fourth Gospel knew the special relationship Jesus had with God; knew how he went off by himself to commune with God; knew his devotion to God that guided his every move. Out of that awareness of the relationship of Jesus with God, the writer of the Fourth Gospel felt able to compose the prayer as *representative* of the close relationship Jesus had with his heavenly Father-God. Accordingly, Jesus prayed aloud, not to bring Lazarus out of the tomb, but "for the sake of the crowd ... so that they may believe that you [Father-God] sent me." For my part, the act of bringing Lazarus out of the tomb after being dead four days would be more than enough to convince me, or the crowd, that Jesus had the power of God on his side.

The stone now rolled away from the tomb, Jesus exclaims his life-giving command: "Lazarus come out." Imagine the scene. Lazarus's feet and hands were tied together with strips of cloth, and his face also covered. How he managed to come out in such a condition is puzzling. Jesus then instructs the helpers to "unbind him and let him go" (11:44). The image of bondage is not incidental. Lazarus's death, like every other death before or after his, signals humanity's bondage to mortality. The *sign* challenges the human condition of sickness, age, and death. The *sign* also holds out a promise of life no longer subject to the ravages of time and disease. Let us be clear: the recalling of Lazarus from the tomb is still a *sign*, not the final reality of eternal life beyond corruption (3:16).

Jesus is the unique forerunner of the latter, represented in his resurrected state among his disciples and friends post-Easter. Those witnesses have handed down their experience of the risen Jesus to generations that followed, to the present time. We cannot brush their experience of the risen Jesus aside as wishful thinking, or flashbacks to his earthly life. Something really happened to motivate them to continue the redemptive work of their Leader on earth. And they paid a price for doing so.

We meet Lazarus one more time in chapter 12. This is the revived Lazarus in his own home, still not saying a word. It was six days before Passover, and "Jesus came to the home of Lazarus, whom he had raised from the dead. There they gave a dinner for him. Martha served, and Lazarus was one of those at the table with [Jesus]" (12:1–2). The event of raising Lazarus created quite a stir down the road in Jerusalem where Jewish leaders guard their Mosaic faith against Messianic uprisings. Accordingly, "a great crowd of the Jews" came to see Lazarus. That attraction did not sit well with the more stringent Jewish leaders, determined to preserve the tradition of Moses. "So the chief priests planned to put Lazarus to death" (12:10). Why would they do such a thing? Because, says the narrator, "it was on account of [Lazarus] that many of the Jews were deserting and were believing in Jesus" (12:10–11).

That statement reflects the situation of the new messianic community of Jesus around the time of writing this Fourth Gospel at the turn of the second century. A significant number of Jewish people were drawn to the new messianic movement, while still hoping to maintain their membership in the Jewish synagogue. Rigid orthodoxy, whether in Judaism or Christianity, will go to great lengths to preserve and protect the long-held traditions through the ages. The next chapter gives a fuller treatment of the tension between the growing messianic community of Jesus and the post-temple Jewish community at Jamnia in Gaza.

We should close this chapter on an upbeat note. Sister Martha served up the dinner, while Jesus reclined at table alongside Lazarus. The reader has to imagine the conversation, because the Fourth Evangelist declines to give a single word from the voice of Lazarus restored. On the sideline, sister Mary opens "a pound of costly perfume made of pure nard, anointed Jesus's feet, and wiped them with her hair. The house was filled with the fragrance of the perfume" (12:3). Where Mary would have found such costly perfume we do not know; nor do we know how she came up with the money to purchase such a commodity. According to the treasurer of the group of disciples, the value was three hundred denarii (12:6). That's about three hundred days' wage for a laborer in Palestine at that time (cf. Matt 20:1–15). Jesus accepted Mary's extravagant gesture of devotion, against the protest of Judas Iscariot. "Leave her alone," Jesus said. "She bought it so that she might keep it for the day of my burial. You always have the poor with you, but you do not always have me" (12:7–8).

9

Concerning "the Jews"

THE FOURTH GOSPEL IS the only book of the New Testament where the term "the Jews" (*hoi Ioudaioi*) appears in abundance. Compared to all three Synoptic Gospels combined, where the label occurs only fourteen times, in the Fourth Gospel "the Jews" appears sixty-nine times. As noted earlier, frequent use of key terms signals the author's interest in what the designation represents. But each use of the term must be assessed on its own merit in context. In a number of cases the term carries a negative hue, while in others it is neutral or positive. Each occurrence has to be analyzed and assessed within its own horizon of history and meaning. One observation can be made with a high degree of certainty. "The Jews" in the Fourth Gospel does not mean every person born into a Jewish family everywhere in the world of the first and second century. Nor does the term mean every Jewish person in the world in good standing in the synagogue. In brief, every occurrence of "the Jews" in the Fourth Gospel should be read and understood strictly within the frame of reference in which the term occurs.

Let's test this approach with reference to a few texts within this Gospel that we have perused already. Recall the case of the parents of the blind man who received his sight in chapter 9. The parents were afraid they would be put out of the synagogue if they confessed Jesus to be the messianic healer of their son. "His parents said this because they were afraid of *the Jews*; for *the Jews* had already agreed that anyone who confessed Jesus to be the Messiah would be put out of the synagogue" (9:22). Observe "the Jews" in italics. The parents themselves were obviously Jewish, but they did not

Concerning "the Jews"

belong to the group of *the Jews* who were interrogating them. The parents valued their membership in the Jewish synagogue, and thus let their son answer for himself. The same Jewish parents were thus afraid of *the Jews*. Does this mean they were afraid of all Jewish people around the world of the time? Of course not. So "the Jews" in this context represents a particular group of Jewish *leaders* responsible for maintaining sound theological and biblical coherence among the members of the synagogue.

We may assume these particular Jews were an educated class from among the many Jewish people in the world of the day. They were able to read and interpret the Hebrew Bible in light of a long tradition anchored in Moses and the Law. And they were also able to determine who was veering off from that treasured Jewish tradition. We may acknowledge further that these particular Jews were not in favor of members of the synagogue heralding *messianic claims*, as some Jews were doing when this Gospel was written with respect to Jesus Messiah.

Now let's shift to a different text and context where "the Jews" are not painted with the same brushstroke. The setting is the death and revivification of Lazarus of Bethany. "When Jesus saw [Mary] weeping, and *the Jews* who came with her also weeping, he was greatly disturbed in spirit and deeply moved (11:33) . . . So *the Jews* said, 'See how he loved him!' (11:36) . . . . Many of *the Jews* therefore, who had come with Mary and had seen what Jesus did, believed in him" (11:45). Clearly, "the Jews" in italics here are not of the same mind as those Jewish leaders interrogating the blind man and his parents in chapter 9. Hence, every time "the Jews" comes up in the Fourth Gospel, the reader has to try to determine as far as possible the particular identity of "the Jews." And the reader of the Fourth Gospel also has to keep in mind that the earliest followers of Jesus were all of Jewish descent, as was Jesus himself. As time went by, the "Christian," or "Messianic," movement from within Judaism flourished, and some of the synagogue people were drawn to the good news the "Christians" were preaching. One such Jewish man was the apostle Paul. At first he was a persecutor of the followers of Jesus-Messiah, but then caught a vision of this Messiah that changed his orientation. So the persecutor became the persecuted. Of course, the Fourth Gospel was written about four decades after Paul's letters. But the issue of proper Jewish identity remained within the synagogue hierarchy through the years, which did not include a Messiah. Yet the new Jewish *messianic* movement also continued to honor their leader, Jesus. By the end of the first century, when the Fourth Gospel was written, the tension between synagogue (*synagōgê* = "a gathering together") and church (*ekklêsia* = "a called-out group") had reached a high-water mark.

This point leads us directly into the double socioreligious context of the Fourth Gospel. The time has come to lay out the *two literary-historical contexts* more pointedly, and then attempt to demonstrate in more detail how the two function in achieving the stated purpose of the Fourth Evangelist in guiding his community in the messianic path: "Now Jesus performed many similar signs in the presence of his followers, which have not been written on this scroll. But these stand written *so that* you may continue to believe that Jesus is the Messiah, the son of God, and that by believing you may have life in his name" (20:30–31, my translation).

PHARISEES AND PRIESTS

The magnificent temple of the Jews that King Herod I built on Mount Zion in Jerusalem prevailed for about ninety years (19 BCE–70 CE). This was the temple Jesus frequented during Jewish festivals. The same temple became the focal point for Jewish worshipers from Palestine, and from elsewhere in the Roman world. *The priests* were the custodians responsible for its upkeep and its worship rituals. *The Pharisees* devoted themselves to teaching sound Jewish doctrine with respect to the Law and the temple service. The basic sense of the term, "Pharisee," is "separated." That is, Pharisees devoted themselves to an authentic interpretation of the law of Moses for the time and situation in which the Jewish people lived. They also sought to ensure that the synagogues within the homeland and beyond kept faith with the Jewish Law and tradition.

These two principal groups within Judaism should not be confused, any more than Christian Baptists and Christian Catholics within Christianity. The Jewish Pharisees and the Jewish priests had different interests and responsibilities, and also somewhat different theology. The Pharisees held a doctrine of resurrection, for example, while the priests did not. The Pharisees adopted a larger canon of Hebrew Scripture than that of the priests. Yet both parties were Jewish. Their central tenet was the efficacy of the teaching in the five scrolls of the Law revealed by *Yahweh*/God to and through the patriarch Moses.

SADDUCEES

It is worth noting that the Jewish group, known as "Sadducees," is not mentioned as such in the Fourth Gospel. In the Synoptic Gospels, however, they do come through a number of times. They were a significant body within Judaism until the destruction of the temple in 70 CE. Unlike the Pharisees, the Sadducees did not believe in resurrection or angels or an after-life. Their focus was on the law of Moses and the importance of temple worship. It was from this group that the various priests of the temple were chosen, including the high priest. It may be that the Fourth Evangelist used the term "priests" specifically as those who had been elected to the office of "priest" in the temple. It also seems reasonable, however, to believe that the Fourth Evangelist used the term "priests" broadly as those leaders who belonged to the Jewish party known from the Synoptic Gospels as "Sadducees," the party from which priests were selected for service in the temple.

THE WAR OF 66–70 CE

It's hard to know exactly what sparked the Roman military invasion of Jewish Palestine in 66 CE. Some Pharisees may have been drawn into a Jewish resistance movement at the time. But the Pharisees by and large were content to teach the Law and support the temple service. By contrast, a group of Jewish Zealots sought to organize a resistance movement against the domination of Rome over the Jewish people in their own traditional land. Roman army general, Titus, organized a cohort of able-bodied soldiers to march on Palestine in the year 66 CE. A Jewish resistance movement believed their God was on their side, and would surely deliver the elect people from the Roman oppressor. That did not happen. General Titus and his military cohorts marched south to the central hotbed of Jewish resistance, the Holy City of Jerusalem.

Flavius Josephus, late-first-century Jewish historian, wrote a detailed account of the five-year Roman war against the Jewish people in Palestine. His large volume, divided into seven books, gives a detailed account of the devastation of the land, and especially of the city of Jerusalem and its people. His graphic account of the destruction of the temple and the Holy City of Jerusalem is chilling. He pictures the blood of the Jewish victims of the Roman war running down the streets of Jerusalem like a river. The war ended in 70 CE. The magnificent temple that King Herod I had built for the Jewish people lay in ruins. Only a partial wall remains to this day. That western wall stands in the Old City of Jerusalem. It is a place of prayer today, also called the Wailing Wall.

A Complicated Love Story

JUDAISM RECONSTITUTED POST-70

Neither the priests nor the Pharisees could withstand the might of the Roman legions. So they were forced to surrender to the foreign power. The priests, and the larger body of Sadducees from which they came, disbanded. In the absence of the temple they lost their ruling seat of power. The Pharisees, by contrast, were teachers of the Law, rabbis who posed limited threat to the peace of Rome (*Pax Romana*). So the Romans permitted the Pharisees, under the able leadership of Johanan ben Zakkai, to set up a Jewish teaching headquarters again in the small town of Jamnia in Gaza. The rabbis of Jamnia established themselves as the ruling rabbis of the Jewish people. Johanan ben Zakkai came up with a number of enactments (called *Takkanoth*) applicable to Jewish people worshiping in synagogues everywhere. The influence of this notable rabbi at Jamnia spread to all Jewish settlements in the Roman world. The purpose was to preserve Jewish tradition and identity as handed down through the Jewish Scripture and oral tradition. Johanan ben Zakkai was also a significant contributor to the Mishnah, which informs the Jewish people of their heritage and obligation to this day. Modern Judaism owes a great deal to this learned rabbi, and to the rabbinic academy over which he presided.

Prayer was central to worship in the newly organized community at Jamnia. One prayer in particular eventually became the centerpiece of synagogue worship. It was called the Eighteen Benedictions, one of which was the prayer relating to heretics (*Minim*). Heretics were those Jewish people who veered away from the course of teaching promulgated by the rabbis of Jamnia. Jewish Christians, such as those implicit in the Fourth Gospel, were prime targets of the prayer against heretics. Jewish members of *the church* continued to use the Jewish Scriptures, the same Scriptures used in the synagogues. But members of *the church* adopted the messiahship of Jesus, which the rabbis at Jamnia deemed heretical. Jewish "heretics" were thereby excommunicated from worship in the synagogue.

A rabbi named Gamaliel came to power in Jamnia at about 80 CE, and ruled until 115 CE, the period within which the Fourth Gospel was written. In his time of rule, the Eighteen Benedictions were formalized, and one benediction accented: *the benediction relating to heretics*. Presumably, this benediction was not simply for those of the rabbinic academy at Jamnia, but for use in synagogues far and wide. For Judaism to maintain its identity as the distinct people of *Yahweh*-God required leadership and direction for living within certain theological and practical parameters. Heretics were not outsiders, as in gentiles. They were Jewish worshipers who failed to observe the rules and beliefs set out by the Jewish rabbinic teachers at Jamnia. More specifically, heretics adopted some points of doctrine that the rabbinic academy could not endorse. When the Eighteen Benedictions were prayed in the synagogues, heretics were cited as outsiders who no longer had a place in the worship service of the synagogue.

The messianic community of Jesus, as reflected in the Fourth Gospel, had within its ranks Jewish people who doubtless thought of themselves as authentic Jews who followed the teaching of another rabbi, namely Jesus Messiah. They would have considered themselves still eligible to attend synagogue services at will. But recall the rabbis at Jamnia appear to have rejected the messianic message coming out of the community of Jesus at the end of the first century. This scenario seems best suited to the situation depicted in chapter 9 where the once-blind man was driven out of the synagogue (9:34), and his parents also were afraid of being expelled (9:22). Similarly, "many, even of the authorities, believed in [Jesus]. But because of the Pharisees [viz. rabbis?] they did not confess it, for fear that they would be put out of the synagogue" (12:42). These "Pharisees" fit the profile of the leading rabbis of Jamnia who sanctioned the praying of the Eighteen Benedictions in which heretics were depicted and subject to expulsion from the synagogue.

Where does this compressed explanation of the Jewish setting of the Fourth Gospel lead us? Simply put, it leads us to an interweaving of two historical-literary settings in the Fourth Gospel. One depicts the time of the ministry of the historical Jesus (ca. 27–30 CE), while the other comes from the turn of the century when members of the community of Jesus Messiah would have been viewed by the rabbis of Jamnia as heretics (ca. 85–110 CE). As conscientious interpreters of the Fourth Gospel, we ignore these two settings to our peril. Recall the Evangelist's closing purpose statement at the end of chapter 20: "These [signs] stand written *so that* you may continue to believe that Jesus is the Messiah, the son of God, and that by believing you may have life in his name." As I read this, the inference is that Jewish members of the community of Jesus Messiah represented in this Gospel have come under pressure to abandon their belief in Jesus Messiah. Otherwise they would be declared heretics, and thus excommunicated from membership in the Jewish synagogue where they once worshiped as members in good standing. Such action would lead to a loss of identity and honor for a Jewish person. And that loss was no trifling matter in a honor-shame society of that time and place.

A COMPLICATED LOVE STORY

INDICTMENT OF CERTAIN JEWS WHO ONCE BELIEVED IN JESUS (8:31–59)

We now come upon one of the most puzzling parts of the Fourth Gospel. At least that's how it appears to me. The whole text runs from 8:31 through 8:59. Within the bounds of this chapter, we shall have to content ourselves with selecting key texts for close reading.

The whole passage focuses on another group, again called "the Jews." In this text we find Jesus leveling vitriolic speech against the group, as nowhere else in the entire Gospel. Imagine being one of the number of very religious Jews who worship God the Father listening to these biting words from Jesus: "If God were your Father, you would love me . . . You are from your father the devil, and you choose to do your father's desires. He was a murderer from the beginning and does not stand in the truth, because there is no truth in him. When he lies, he speaks according to his own nature, for he is a liar and the father of lies" (8:44). In enlightened society this statement, without context, could be construed as grossly anti-Semitic. But that would be a serious misunderstanding. Remember Jesus was a Jew, and all the earliest believers in "the church" likewise Jews. That is why Christians have continued to own and study the Bible of the Jewish people to this day. (Christians call it the "Old Testament"). So we are obliged to ask what led to this strong denouncement of these particular Jews.

A good clue comes from the opening line of this pericope as follows: "Then Jesus said to *the Jews who had believed in him*, 'If you continue in my word, you are truly my disciples; and you will know the truth, and the truth will make you free'" (8:31–32). We have here a much-quoted line: "the truth will make you free" (I knew a good man who made this saying his motto for life. His family had the saying chiseled onto his headstone). But this one important saying about truth should not stand alone. It belongs to a worthy commendation to this group of Jews who had believed in Jesus. The response from this group of Jews to Jesus, however, is one of correction. "We are descendants of Abraham and have never been slaves to anyone. What do you mean by saying, 'You will be made free'?" (8:33). Suddenly the reader senses that the Jewish converts who had once believed in Jesus have returned to their sacred Jewish history and practice. In short, they appear to have discontinued their belief in the word of Jesus (8:43). Hence the sudden turn of thought in the voice of Jesus from one of *commendation* to one of *bitter censure*: "You are from your father the devil, and you choose to do your father's desires. He was a murderer from the beginning and does not stand in the truth, because there is no truth in him" (8:44).

Now let's consider a likely historical context for this strange turn of thought. As discussed above, in the aftermath of the destruction of the temple both rabbinic Judaism and the messianic community of the Jewish Jesus represented in this Gospel forged ahead. We have learned already that the new Judaism shunned messianic claims in their synagogue. For one thing, such claims could bring down the wrath of Rome again. A Messiah is traditionally one anointed to kingship. Roman political leaders will have nothing of that. So the rabbinic leaders at Jamnia have declared all such belief and practice heretical. That would mean anyone wishing to keep ties with the synagogue would have to abandon any connection with messianic evangelists and their communities. Simply put, good standing with the *synagogue* means no standing with the *church* that heralds Jesus as Messiah. All of this was happening when this Fourth Gospel was written. To be expelled from synagogue worship was a grievous experience for upstanding Jewish people who valued their rich religious heritage.

In conclusion, I view the language and thought of this section of the Fourth Gospel, 8:31–59, to reflect a situation in the life of the community that first received this Gospel at the beginning of the second century CE. A group of Jewish believers in Jesus Messiah sought to continue worship in the traditional synagogue, only to find themselves branded as heretics. A choice had to be made. Deny their affiliation with the new community of Jesus Messiah and return to the synagogue worship, or continue in the new community of Jesus Messiah and be banned shamefully from synagogue. Under the rule of the Jewish academy at Jamnia they could not affirm both the new messianic movement of Jesus and the traditional worship in the synagogue. So we appear to have a group of "the Jews," cited in 8:31, who once upon a time declared faith in Jesus Messiah, and then later abandoned their former confession to become reestablished in the traditional Jewish synagogue. Hence the deeply troubling language in the voice of Jesus aimed at those who abandoned their new messianic faith in deference to the traditional synagogue service and its leaders.

10

Jesus's Inauspicious Entrance into Jerusalem for Passover

Passover was and is a weeklong festival in Judaism. It celebrates deliverance from slavery by the grace and power of Israel's God. Being Jewish, Jesus doubtless celebrated a number of Passovers during his thirty-year life in Palestine. But this one was different from the others in several respects, as we shall see shortly. He had become well-known and highly regarded by the rank and file in Galilee and Judea according to the testimony in all four Gospels (12:12–15; Mark 11:4–10; Matt 21:6–10; Luke 19:30–38). The event of Jesus's final entrance into the Holy City of Jerusalem deserves to be explored as far as possible through the lens of the first-century Jewish audience, and not least among those in positions of power in Jerusalem.

I propose to highlight five features that stand out in all four Gospels, with some variation from one to the other. Each Gospel writer had his own way of setting forth the action and reaction. Matthew's rendition is somewhat bizarre, as we shall discover shortly, and is usually not read on the first Sunday of Holy Week. That of the Fourth Evangelist is the most popular in churches, seemingly because of the presence of palm branches in the drama. Let us proceed, then, to the five features depicted in the Fourth Gospel alongside the versions in the three Synoptic Gospels.

Jesus's Inauspicious Entrance into Jerusalem for Passover

THE GREAT CROWD

The people who thronged Jerusalem on the occasion of Passover recorded in 12:12–15 were not gathered principally to see and hear Jesus. They had learned since childhood from synagogue and household about the miraculous emancipation of the ancient Hebrews whom God set free from the social and political clutches of the pharaoh of Egypt long ago. Such a memorial tends to linger long through successive generations, as well it should.

But by the time of this particular Passover the people gathered in Jerusalem had heard about the ministry of Jesus, his healing power and his captivating message about a new kind of deliverance by the grace of the same God that had saved the ancient Hebrews from bondage. His was not a ministry of enslavement to earthly powers, but one of deliverance from physical, spiritual, economic, and political bondage. The Jewish people of Palestine longed for freedom from foreign overlords. Jesus had spoken words of renewal and inheritance, but never words of war by which to achieve these ends. The announcement in his message was one of peace and blessing. "The meek shall inherit the land, and delight themselves in abundant prosperity" (Ps 37:11; cf. Matt 5:5). Peasants with land could make a living from it. But more than a few peasants in Palestine lost their land to wealthy landlords, and were thereby at their mercy. Jesus witnessed the weak and the sick in the land of promise and had compassion on them.

The word and work of Jesus had preceded him in Jerusalem on that Passover week. So when the Passover crowd heard that Jesus was in the vicinity, they made a point of finding him to observe his action and hear his word of life and peace. The crowd of Jewish people who gathered made their presence known in their shouts of joy and hope, and in their symbolic action toward Jesus. But crowds can be dangerous to the peace of Rome in occupied Palestine. Pilate, along with the Jewish high priest, knew as much, as Jesus discovered before this particular Holy Week was over.

BRANCHES OF PALM TREES

Credit goes to the Fourth Evangelist exclusively for the traditional title ascribed to the first Sunday of Easter week: Palm Sunday. The text simply states that the people nearby "took branches of palm trees and went out to meet [Jesus]" (12:13). It is said that the palm branch symbolized victory and peace in the ancient Near East. In ancient Egypt it represented immortality. Its presence in the story of Jesus's entrance into Jerusalem in the Fourth Gospel probably carries such meaning, but in a paradoxical way. Jesus's mode of transportation is anything but victorious or triumphant. If anything Jesus is turning the usual meaning of triumph on its head, as we shall see shortly.

Meanwhile, we should ask how the story appears in the other three Gospels. Sure enough, Mark and Matthew both paint a picture of the people cutting branches from trees found in nearby fields and spreading the branches on the roadway ahead of Jesus. But such branches are not from palm trees. Palms do not grow in the vicinity of Jerusalem located on a plateau at 754 meters above sea level in the Judean mountains. Palms did grow well in the region of Jericho, which is about 258 meters below sea level. The two Gospels of Mark and Matthew depict ordinary branches found in nearby fields to serve the paradoxical purpose of the humble and peaceable king Jesus. Luke alone of the four evangelists presents a picture of Jesus's entrance into Jerusalem without any branches on the road ahead of Jesus. Instead of spreading branches of any kind, Luke's "people kept spreading their cloaks on the road" (Luke 19:36). There is no way that I can find to harmonize these disparate features of the story from one Gospel to another. By all accounts we can state with confidence that the people knew the goodness and grace of Jesus toward people in need. He lived to save them from hunger and pain and death. So they paid respectful homage to him on this auspicious occasion of Passover in Jerusalem.

HOSANNA!

The word in English rendered "hosanna" has its roots in the Hebrew Bible, especially in the Psalms. Here is a notable example from Psalm 118:25: "Save us, we beseech you, O LORD! / O LORD, we beseech you, give us success!" This is a classic example of Hebrew parallelism where the second line echoes the first. The suppliant prays to Israel's God, uniquely called Yahweh. The plea is for salvation and well-being. Such a prayer implies something is wrong in the society in which the suppliant cries out for help. It would be wrongheaded to suggest that the plea is for an otherworldly salvation. More likely a reigning king in Israel has put the people of the land to work to enhance his court and kingdom, and pays them little for their labor. They and their family may go hungry as a result of paying taxes in support of the elaborate court of the king. Or it may be that the appeal to the Lord is for protection against ruthless invaders of their land. Whatever the harsh situation, "hosanna" is a real cry from an Israelite heart to the Lord God of the universe to make life bearable. By this token it is a peasant plea for a better life for oneself and family. It is not a heart cry from a wealthy king.

The word "hosanna" occurs in three of the four Gospels at the time of Jesus's entry into Jerusalem for his last Passover. Luke does not use the word in his description of the crowd's joyful chants on the occasion of Passover. The gathered crowd of people seem to know about the sympathetic love of Jesus for his people living under foreign rule, and paying taxes to a foreign power in addition to funds for the upkeep of the Jewish temple. Notice the key elements in the people's chant reported in the Fourth Gospel: "Hosanna! Blessed is the one who comes in the name of the Lord—the King of Israel!" (12:13). This is the same Lord to whom the earlier Psalmist cried "hosanna."

And in the people's chant they recognize Jesus as vice-regent on earth to the Lord God of the universe who saves his people. They do not hail the Roman emperor as one who will save them. Nor do they appeal to Rome's representative in Judea, Pontius Pilate. Jesus is one of them, and one with them at this auspicious time of celebration of Passover. They have seen or heard of his compassion and his generosity toward those in need: the widow and orphan, the sick and the sorrowful. Now here they are marching with him into the Holy City of Jerusalem. Little do the chanting people know what will happen to this same Jesus when those in political power get wind of his popularity among the people of the land, and his radical rule of life and love in relation to them.

THE KING OF ISRAEL!

The chant of the people on the occasion of Jesus's entrance into Jerusalem was politically charged. The syntax in the NRSV is somewhat ambiguous. It reads, "Blessed is the one who comes in the name of the Lord—the King of Israel!" (12:13). Is the king of Israel the Lord? Or is the king of Israel the one who comes in the name of the Lord? The text of the Authorized Version of 1611 is transparently unambiguous: "Blessed is the King of Israel that cometh in the name of the Lord." Accordingly, "the King of Israel" is Jesus of Nazareth, the "blessed" one entering Jerusalem "in the name of the Lord." Either way the shout of jubilation is politically charged. There was no king in Israel at the time. The last king of all Israel was the ruthless Herod I, the one in power at the time of Jesus's birth. Herod I (otherwise called Herod the Great) made an appeal to the Roman Caesar to appoint him ruler of Judea. Herod won the position and eventually ruled all of Palestine from 37–4 BCE as a Roman client king.

When Jesus entered Jerusalem for Passover there was no king of Israel. But according to the people's shouts of jubilation at his coming the crowd saw in him the kind of king they would welcome. He was humble, as they were. He would rule with the people of the land, not rule over them as a prestigious monarch. But the power of Rome was still a force to be reckoned with in the land of Palestine. The people's shouts about the kingship of Jesus would eventually reach the ears of the ones in power in the Jewish Sanhedrin, and not least in Pilate's ears, as we shall discover in a later chapter. What needs to be acknowledged is that Jesus did not silence the crowd on the subject of his kingship. Similarly, as we shall discover later, Jesus did not deny the inference in Pilate's question to Jesus, "So you are a king?" (18:37). If I were to pinpoint one element in particular that led to the trial of Jesus it would be this: his teaching about the kingdom of God and his kingly role in bringing it to fruition.

RIDING ON A YOUNG DONKEY (ZECH 9:9)

We begin this part of the story of Jesus's inauspicious entrance into Jerusalem at the beginning of Passover week as we did the other parts: giving priority to the account in the Fourth Gospel. A comparison with the other three Gospels will follow.

Jesus did not own a donkey by all accounts, and accordingly did not ride on one from Galilee to Jerusalem. But he "found a young donkey and sat on it" (12:13). It was a deliberate act, presumably also a symbolic one. It wasn't a matter of being tired after the long walk south from Galilee. The point was that he would ride the donkey into the Holy City of David to make a point. But what was the point? The donkey was principally a humble beast of burden at the time, as it is still in a number of countries. (When I was in Bolivia I saw donkeys loaded with two full bags of heavy material slung over their backs as they climbed up a hillside.) At the time of Jesus in Palestine the humble donkey was the animal of peasants, not that of kings and courtiers. I doubt that Pilate would ride a humble donkey from Caesarea to Jerusalem to oversee the Jewish Passover.

Jesus's Inauspicious Entrance into Jerusalem for Passover

But even more to the point, Jesus doubtless knew the poetic text of Zech 9:9 and enacted it on this occasion of Passover, which celebrates the salvation of the enslaved Hebrews in Egypt.

> Rejoice greatly, O daughter Zion!
> > Shout aloud, O daughter Jerusalem!
> Lo, your king comes to you;
> > triumphant and victorious is he,
> humble and riding on a donkey,
> > on a colt, the foal of a donkey.

Here again is a classic example of Hebrew poetry where a second line echoes the previous one. There were not two donkeys, but two poetic lines carrying the same theme in related terms of reference. There is also irony in this background text of Zech 9:9. The king that rides into Jerusalem on the back of a donkey is "triumphant and victorious," yet "humble and riding on a donkey." So there is no need for the people of Jerusalem to fear such a triumphant yet humble king.

We come now to a comparison between the Fourth Gospel's rendering of Jesus's ride on the back of a donkey and that of the three Synoptic Gospels. It should be noted again that most present-day scholars agree that the Gospel of Mark is the earliest, and that Matthew and Luke drew on Mark's material in the composition of their own. The story of Jesus's entrance into Jerusalem on a donkey is a case in point. But as we shall see again, Matthew and Luke shape the material they find in Mark as they see fit. For our purposes two points will suffice.

(1) In all three Synoptic Gospels the instruction from Jesus about bringing a donkey to him is virtually the same. Jesus seems to know, either intuitively or from previous experience, where the disciples will find a donkey for him to ride into Jerusalem (Matt 21:1–3; Mark 11:1–6; Luke 19:29–34). In the Fourth Gospel, however, Jesus fetches the donkey himself (12:14).

(2) Of the three synoptic authors Matthew is the only one to misinterpret the Hebrew parallelism in Zechariah 9:9. The resulting image in Matthew becomes absurd: "The disciples went and did as Jesus had directed them; they brought *the donkey and the colt*, and put their cloaks on *them*, and he [Jesus] sat on *them*" (Matt 21:6–7). It stretches imagination to visualize Jesus straddling both animals. The writer of Matthew simply misread

the Hebrew genre of poetic parallelism. As with Mark and Luke, however, the Fourth Gospel has Jesus riding only one donkey.

To conclude, Jesus's action in finding and riding a donkey into Jerusalem on an auspicious Jewish holiday with crowds cheering him on was calculated. It is important to keep in mind the peaceable image of Jesus on a humble donkey riding into the highly regarded city of Jerusalem, otherwise known as the city of King David. It begs the question of Jesus's identity and his purpose in acting as he did on this special holiday. According to Mark, no sooner had Jesus entered Jerusalem on a donkey to shouts of triumph than he entered the temple (Mark 11:11). The temple was large and ornate, built by Herod the Great over the course of many years. Herod's vision, seemingly, was to match the glory of Solomon's temple, sparing no manpower or finances in the process. The dramatic irony of Jesus riding into the Holy City on a lowly donkey to the cheers of the people, and then entering the magnificent temple shortly thereafter, was boldly transparent.

11

The Beloved Disciple in the Spotlight

As we have observed together so far, there are four recognizable parts to the Fourth Gospel in this order: *Prologue* (1:1–18), *Book of Signs* (1:19—12:50), *Book of the Passion* (13:1—20:31), and *Appendix* (21:1–25). Between the Prologue and the Appendix sit the two principal parts of the treatise. Now one might expect to find in these two significant blocks of material a complete list of the names of the twelve disciples that Jesus chose as his inner circle. Not so. We have to resort to the three Synoptic Gospels to find the given names of the Twelve. Granted, the symbolic term, "the Twelve," does appear three times in the Fourth Gospel, but without an inkling of the personal identity of the members (6:67, 70; 20:24). Jesus's choice of *twelve men* was doubtless deliberate. The number probably signals a restored Israel underway in the kingdom ministry of Jesus in the traditional land of promise.

In the Fourth Gospel only two names from the Twelve are cited as belonging to that select group: Judas Iscariot (6:70) and Thomas the twin (20:24). We recognize three other followers of Jesus from the list of Twelve in Matthew, Mark, and Luke: Simon Peter, Andrew, and Philip. Oddly enough, the Fourth Evangelist does not cite these as belonging to "the Twelve." Then there is Nathanael, who became a faithful follower of Jesus. But his name does not appear anywhere in Matthew, Mark, or Luke, much less in the lists of the Twelve. In the Fourth Gospel, Nathanael's testimony to Jesus qualifies him boldly as a faithful disciple: "Rabbi, you are the Son of God! You are the King of Israel!" (1:49; 21:2)

A Complicated Love Story

Beside all of these known disciples of Jesus stands one very special disciple shrouded in anonymity in the Fourth Gospel: "the disciple whom [Jesus] loved" (18:12; 20:2). This one, clearly identified as special to Jesus, enters the drama in the second main part of this Gospel: the Book of the Passion. And this enigmatic figure then remains in sharp focus to the very end of the story. Here are ten points gleaned from the material in the Book of the Passion and Appendix, discussed in more detail below.

1. Jesus loves one disciple uniquely (13:23; 19:26; 20:2; 21:7, 20)
2. This beloved disciple is anonymous in the Fourth Gospel
3. He mediates between Peter and Jesus during the last Passover meal (13:23–25)
4. Known to the high priest, he accompanied Jesus to the court of trial (18:15)
5. The woman gatekeeper at the temple obeyed the anonymous disciple, and thereby granted Peter access to the court (18:16)
6. He stands firmly with Jesus at the time of trial, while Peter denies his discipleship to Jesus (18:17–18)
7. He accepts responsibility for the mother of Jesus (19:27)
8. He outruns Peter to the tomb where the body of Jesus had been placed (20:4)
9. He experienced the resurrected presence of Jesus, and enlightened Peter that the persona was indeed that of "the Lord" (21:7)
10. He stands aside while the resurrected Jesus tests the genuineness of Peter's love (21:15–20)

I hold these ten points to be self-evident within the Fourth Gospel, which includes the appendix in chapter 21. Yet they beg explanation beyond the bare facts, which they shall have forthwith. We are then left with the question of the given name of this enigmatic figure in the second part of this Gospel. That question I shall treat in the second half of the chapter. In the meantime, let's ponder further each of the ten observations listed above.

The Beloved Disciple in the Spotlight

MAKING SENSE OF THE TEN OBSERVATIONS

1. Jesus loved one disciple in particular. If it was well-known among the group of disciples that Jesus loved one of them above the rest, it is astonishing that the others took that matter in stride. (I was the youngest of a family of nine children. I can't imagine our parents making it known that one child was loved above the other eight.) There must have been something inherently different in the nameless disciple that led to this designation. I have no doubt that Jesus loved all of his followers. Yet this one stands out above and beyond all the others. And the rest seem to accept that reality without dispute. What would make this nameless disciple more lovable? What would lead the Fourth Evangelist to highlight this disciple boldly in the Book of the Passion of Jesus? And why is this beloved disciple of Jesus set up vis-à-vis Peter specifically? We shall put these queries on hold for the moment. Suffice it to say that there existed a special love-relationship between Jesus and one disciple in particular, who seems not to have been a member of the twelve.

2. The anonymity with which this disciple is treated in the Fourth Gospel is astonishing. He comes across as a privileged and knowledgeable figure in the Book of the Passion. Such important figures in history have proper, given names. Imagine, for a moment, Alexander the Great being known only as "the general that Philip II loved." Something kept the Fourth Evangelist from naming this unique disciple. Some have argued that his given name is absent because he was the writer of this Gospel, and humbly concealed his nominal identity as the beloved disciple of Jesus. This matter will be explored in more detail below. Meanwhile, let it be clear that the anonymity is no accident, nor an oversight. It is deliberate and should be respected and interpreted as such. Moreover, it would not be appropriate to adopt without question the name of this special disciple put forward by church leaders for the first time at the end of second century, and then adopted carte blanche by the larger church thereafter down to the present time. The anonymity in the Fourth Gospel is purposeful and deliberate. But the *rationale* for the anonymity in the second part the Fourth Gospel is not given. I aim to offer a proposal about the identity of this anonymous figure towards the end of this chapter, to be tested by the reader.

3. The disciple Jesus loved mediates a critical matter between Peter and Jesus during what appears to be a Passover meal. Picture a large low table, perhaps about eighteen inches above ground, with the participants *reclining* next to each other during the meal. (They were not sitting on chairs around a modern table.) Jesus was hosting the Passover meal, and the disciple Jesus loved was reclining next to him. Peter was puzzled by a comment Jesus made about one of the disciples betraying him. So Peter asked that other disciple to find out which disciple Jesus had in mind as the betrayer. What is evident from this episode during the meal is that Peter is in a secondary position to that of the disciple Jesus loved. First, the beloved disciple is physically closer to Jesus than his counterpart, Peter. Second, Peter seems to believe that the beloved disciple will have a better chance of eliciting an apt response from Jesus about the betrayer in the group. This is the first glimpse into the two-sided relationship of this special disciple. On the one hand Jesus relates lovingly to this anonymous disciple, and on the other Peter's discipleship and leadership take second place to the character and leadership of the beloved disciple. It strikes me, therefore, that the Fourth Evangelist knew something of the history between these two figures in the developing community of Jesus Messiah after Jesus's death. And with help from the writings of the apostle Paul and the book of Acts we know something of that history as well.

4. The beloved disciple outranks Peter in terms of temple politics. The trial of Jesus was conducted in a court of the temple. Not everyone was permitted into that quarter, beyond the ones who were trying the case. The anonymous disciple and Peter followed Jesus as far as possible toward the court of trial in the temple precincts. But this special disciple was given entrance into the court, while Peter was obliged to stand outside at the gate. "Simon Peter and another disciple followed Jesus. Since that disciple was known to the high priest, he went with Jesus into the courtyard of the high priest" (18:15). Whatever his identity, this nameless disciple of Jesus had political clout with the temple authorities that Peter lacked. How he acquired such status is something of a mystery. From what we know of the twelve disciples, none of them hailed from wealth or political advantage. Four of them were fishermen when Jesus called them to be his followers: brothers Peter and Andrew, and brothers James and John. Given their trade as fishermen on the Sea of Galilee, and their subsequent discipleship to

The Beloved Disciple in the Spotlight

Jesus, it would be hard to imagine any one of these four having the kind of connection with the temple authorities that the anonymous disciple had. Remarkably, this disciple had the ear of the high priest, on the one hand, and the special love of Jesus on the other.

5. Peter was obliged to stop at a gate leading to the court of the temple. A woman was commissioned to guard the gate against intruders. Peter was deemed to be one. He lacked the political connection with the high priest. Here is where the other anonymous disciple comes on the scene with authority to bring Peter into the court to witness the trial. "So the other disciple, who was known to the high priest, went out, spoke to the woman who guarded the gate, and brought Peter in" (18:16). Clearly, the disciple whom Jesus loved has connections that Peter lacks. Unlike Peter, the special disciple has the authority from the high priest to judge who may or may not be admitted to the court. Who is this very privileged person? He is certainly no ordinary disciple of Jesus. He is faithful to Jesus, on the one hand, and privileged to have the support of the high priest, on the other. I find this scenario nothing short of a conundrum begging resolution.

6. There is not the slightest hint of betrayal or denial of Jesus from the beloved disciple. But Peter's stance is quite another matter. When the anonymous disciple comes to the gate with authority to bring Peter into the court, the woman at the gate quizzed Peter about his affiliation with Jesus. "The woman said to Peter, 'You are not also one of this man's disciples, are you?' He said, 'I am not'" (18:17). Flat-out denial from Peter. Presumably he was trying to save himself from recrimination, or worse, crucifixion. For whatever reason, the disciple so beloved by Jesus, and so faithful to him, escapes judgment from the Jewish court. And by the account in the Fourth Gospel, this special disciple remained with Jesus during his suffering and death on the cross. None of the other disciples are listed as being present at the ignominious scene (19:25–27).

7. This beloved disciple stands with the women at the foot of the cross, and remains devoted to Jesus to the end. As noted in a previous chapter, Jesus handed over the responsibility for his mother's welfare to this disciple (19:27). Jesus's father had died earlier. In that society the responsibility for the welfare of a widowed mother fell to the eldest son. It is generally held that Jesus was Mary's firstborn son. But now

with Jesus's earthly life ebbing to a close he is justly concerned for the well-being of his mother. So he transfers filial responsibility for his mother to this special disciple. The terms of the transfer are formal and binding. "When Jesus saw his mother and the disciple whom he loved standing beside her, he said to his mother, 'Woman, here is your son.' Then he said to the disciple, 'Here is your mother.' And from that hour the disciple took her into his own home" (19:26–27). Two observations should be made at this point. First, if the mother of Jesus marginally knew this disciple, it seems strange that Jesus would make such a transfer. Second, it seems even stranger that the son next in age after Jesus would abandon his mother. Surely the mother of Jesus would feel more at home under the care and support of another of her sons! Were her sons heartless children? (Cf. Acts 1:14c, where the mother of Jesus was with her sons in an upstairs room in Jerusalem a short time after the crucifixion.)

8. Apparently the beloved disciple was a better runner than Peter. When Mary Magdalene brought news of the empty tomb to the beloved disciple and Peter, the two men ran to the tomb to witness the scene for themselves. The detail about running to the tomb provides yet another opportunity to accent the prowess of the beloved disciple over that of Peter. "Then Peter and the other disciple set out and went toward the tomb. The two were running together, but the other disciple outran Peter and reached the tomb first" (20:3–4). The significance of this athletic detail is scarcely earth-shattering. Is it that Peter's athletic ability was weaker than that of the other disciple? Or could it be that Peter's interest in discovering something more about the crucified Jesus falls short of that of the beloved disciple? The latter is a possibility. I think it is yet another way for the Fourth Evangelist to accent the stature and stamina of the nameless disciple over that of Peter. When Peter reached the empty tomb he walked in and simply observed the linen wrappings. "Then the other disciple, who reached the tomb first, also went in, and he saw and *believed*" (20:8). In every way the beloved disciple outperforms Peter, especially in terms of faithfulness and dependability.

9. In the Appendix the risen Jesus appeared by the Sea of Galilee, "but the disciples did not know that it was Jesus" (21:4). The beloved disciple was the first to recognize the persona of the resurrected Jesus. That disciple then enlightened Peter that this persona was truly that

The Beloved Disciple in the Spotlight

of "the Lord," implying that it required special insight to recognize the resurrected form of Jesus. But here's another interesting tidbit about Peter that the author of the Appendix felt at liberty to disclose. "When Simon Peter heard that it was the Lord, he put on some clothes, for he was naked, and jumped into the sea" (21:7). It seems that at every turn Peter is shown up to be an erratic individual. Why he would be walking around openly naked is peculiar. It is even more peculiar that he would put on clothes before jumping into the Sea of Tiberius. But the text implies motivation for doing so: he didn't want to be found naked in the presence of the Lord, Jesus. Again, there appears to be a penchant even in the Appendix to show Peter to be a less worthy disciple than the nameless one that Jesus loved.

10. Chapter 21 features the same two characters, Peter and the beloved disciple, in relation to the resurrected Jesus. But this time Peter's relationship to Jesus is critically tested (21:15–20). All the while, the other disciple that Jesus loved stands to the side effectively not needing to have his love for Jesus questioned or tested. Apparently this other disciple basks in the love of Jesus, and thus reciprocates in kind. Before moving forward to the three stages of the test, it would be well to set out the specific terms of the test.

In most English versions of the Bible, including the NRSV, the key verb "to love" at the heart of the test is identical in spelling with Jesus's question and in Peter's response. Why, then, the need to ask Peter the identical question three times? The second two become thereby redundant in the English translation. The fact is that the *Greek word* Jesus used for "love" is different from Peter's Greek word for "love." And the difference makes the questioning acute. The Greek spelling behind two of the English verbs that Jesus asks Peter is *not* the same as the verb in Peter's response. To suggest that the meaning is essentially the same between the two different words is to miss the point of their respective places in the dialogue. Let me illustrate, using the Greek form, but in English script (21:15–17):

1. <u>Jesus to Peter</u>: "Simon son of John, do you love [*agapās*] me more than these?"
   <u>Peter to Jesus</u>: "Yes, Lord; you know that I love [*philō*] you."
2. <u>Jesus to Peter</u>: "Simon son of John, do you love [*agapās*] me?"
   <u>Peter to Jesus</u>: "Yes, Lord; you know that I love [*philō*] you."

3. <u>Jesus to Peter</u>: "Simon son of John, do you love [*philō*] me?"
   <u>Peter to Jesus</u>: "Lord, you know everything; you know that I love [*philō*] you."

Notice the difference in spelling in the verb "to love" in brackets. In the first two questions Jesus uses the same Greek word for "love," *agapās*, while Peter responds using another Greek word for "love," *philō*. Then in the third question Jesus uses Peter's word, *philō*. When Peter heard Jesus use his word, "Peter felt hurt because he said to him the third time, 'Do you love [*philō*] me?'" (21:17). Why would Peter feel hurt when Jesus used Peter's word for "love"? The most obvious answer is: because Jesus moved from the more demanding word for "love," *agapaō*, to the less demanding word that Peter used. Jesus's word demands a willingness to go to any length for the sake of the loved one. Peter's word, however, implies friendship when circumstances are conducive to such a friendly relationship. Recall Peter's denial of Jesus.

Meanwhile, the other disciple whom Jesus loved is nearby, and is not questioned by Jesus. That leads Peter to encourage Jesus to do the same to the other disciple. "When Peter saw him, he said to Jesus, 'Lord, what about him?' Jesus said to [Peter], 'If it is my will that he remain until I come, what is that to you? Follow me!'" (21:21–22).

A NARRATOR'S COMMENT

We have found a third-person narrator's hand in other parts of the Fourth Gospel, so also here in the brief conclusion to the Appendix (21:24–25). The conclusion to the Appendix is not necessarily the conclusion to the twenty chapters preceding. That conclusion, as we have seen, urges the reader to be faithful in honoring Jesus as Savior-Messiah, and in doing so find eternal life (20:30–31). The unidentified disciple that we met in the Book of the Passion is presumably the same figure focused also in chapter 21. But he is still unidentified in the concluding comment. His testimony is highlighted, to be sure, and his behavior unblemished. But his objective identity remains shrouded in mystery.

The third-party narrator in the Appendix also slips in a tantalizing phrase, the significance of which has run the gamut. Note the tiny phrase highlighted in the following sentence: "This is the disciple who is testifying to these things *and has written them*, and we know that his testimony is true" (21:24). Much has been made of this highlighted phrase. For whatever reason, some people believe the third-person narrator who wrote this part of the Appendix is the enigmatic disciple himself. Others suspect it applies only to the Book of the Passion where the disciple whom Jesus loved comes to the foreground. Or maybe "these things" the anonymous disciple is said to have written are limited to the Appendix of chapter 21, which was probably written some time after the twenty chapters preceding. When all is said and done we are still left with an unidentified disciple-figure, one that was very dear to the heart of Jesus. The reason for such affection is not stated boldly. That fact leaves us searching for the sociocultural and familial identity of this outstanding disciple in relation to Jesus on the one hand, and to Peter on the other.

Keep in mind the likelihood that the Fourth Gospel was written in the early part of the second century. Given that deduction about the time of writing this Gospel, it would be far-reaching to attribute the authorship to a disciple of Jesus who followed him in the late twenties of the first century. That would mean the author would have been 90-plus years of age when he wrote the Fourth Gospel, and fluent in Greek. The blunt fact of the matter is that this Gospel does not reveal the identity of its author, or authors. It may well be the product of several hands and minds from the same time frame and the same Christian community in the early second century: a collaborative effort, so to speak. Evidently, the community of Jesus-Messiah was under pressure when this Gospel was written. Its purpose, according to 20:31, was to encourage the beleaguered community of Jesus-Messiah to continue believing in him in the face of pressures of various sorts.

WHO WAS THE SPECIAL DISCIPLE JESUS LOVED? A REASONABLE DEDUCTION

It was customary for Christian church authorities from the late second century to the end of the fourth century to sanction material in scrolls intended for use in Christian communities. These clerics approved the reading of certain material they deemed worthy of Christian worship and teaching in the developing Christian church worldwide, while disapproving others. Many scrolls, such as that of the Fourth Gospel, were originally written anonymously. Some Christians were reading these scrolls prior to official sanction, until the practice was discovered by the ordained clerics. When that happened the official clerics would read the scroll and judge its value for church service. The Fourth Gospel was eventually approved. The process of church sanction of scrolls included the assigning of the name of an apostle, or a close friend of an apostle, as *author* of the scroll. Again, an ordained cleric was assigned the job of attaching a name to the scroll. The Fourth Gospel was assigned the name of "John" the son of Zebedee and apostle of Jesus as the author. This John was then believed to be the disciple Jesus loved.

In 367 CE, Bishop Athanasius of Alexandria wrote an Easter letter to be circulated in the churches. In addition to providing the date of Easter for that year, Athanasius listed twenty-seven documents he deemed worthy for reading in the liturgy of the church. Athanasius used the Greek word *kanōn* (canon = rule, measure) as a ploy for settling the number and names of books that could be used in church liturgy. While the debate about a closed or open canon continued in some quarters, the list that Athanasius drafted constitutes the New Testament of the Christian church to the present time.

Alongside the creation of a New Testament canon was the invention and development of the codex (book) form, which was fully adopted around the same time as the adoption of the canon. In the years prior to the adoption of the book-form, sets of scrolls were kept in containers. That system presented the practical matter of identifying each papyrus scroll within a container. Rather than opening every scroll in the container for identification, the name on a slip of papyrus was attached to the outside of the scroll where the outer edge meets the papyrus. The "slip," as it was called, prevented the scroll from expansion, on the one hand, and identified the scroll for the reader on the other.

In the case of the Fourth Gospel the title on the *outside* slip was simply *kata Iōannên*, "according to John." Henceforth, the content *inside* the scroll became identified with the historical person thus named on the outer slip on the scroll. When that step of attaching a name to the outside of the scroll was adopted, it was thereby assumed that the author of the whole document was the same as the name on the slip. And, as noted above, the few words in 21:24 of the Fourth Gospel about "the disciple who is testifying to these things *and has written them*" was deemed to be none other than John, son of Zebedee, and disciple of Jesus: "the one [disciple] that Jesus loved" (13:23; 20:2).

I contend with conviction that this conclusion, reached long ago and adopted blithely by Christian congregations to this day, lacks reasonable and responsible support from relevant sources.

The Beloved Disciple in the Spotlight

Let's now explore the available sources for evidence of the character and mission of John the son of Zebedee on two fronts: (1) as qualified for the high honor of being "the disciple whom Jesus loved," and (2) as outperforming Peter at every turn. The sources are three, given here in order of composition: Paul's letter to the Galatians, the three Synoptic Gospels, and the Acts of the Apostles.

(1) In Galatians 2:9 the apostle Paul recognizes three leaders of the Jewish church in Jerusalem as "pillars": James, Peter, and John, in that order. Apparently these three earned the title insofar as they guided the Jerusalem community of Jewish Christ-followers through tough times. The order of the names is significant. James the brother of Jesus heads up the list of three (Gal 1:19), followed by Peter and then John. This third position in the list of three hardly qualifies for the stature of "the disciple Jesus loved." His name occurs only at this one place in all the letters of Paul written in the 50s CE. By Paul's account, then, John was not a major player in the group of three, as compared to the stature of James and Peter.

When we peruse the Synoptic Gospels we find John always in third position in the list of the three disciples that Jesus singled out for special duty: Peter, James, and John (Mark 5:37; 9:22; 14:33; Luke 5:10). This James is a son of Zebedee and brother of John. More striking is the bluster that James and John displayed against some Samaritans who refused to welcome Jesus and his followers to their village. The two brothers wanted Jesus to enable them "to command fire to come down from heaven and consume [the Samaritans]." But Jesus "turned and rebuked" James and John (Luke 9:54). No wonder Jesus nicknamed those two brothers "Sons of Thunder" (Mark 3:17).

Does this John measure up to the pristine character of the anonymous figure we meet in the Fourth Gospel? The one whom Jesus loved? Or how about this attitude coming from the same two brothers, James and John? "Teacher, we want you to do for us whatever we ask of you" (Mark 10:35). And what did they request from Jesus? "Grant us to sit, one at your right hand and one at your left, in your glory" (Mark 10:37). Does this John resemble the disciple in the Fourth Gospel whom Jesus loved? The Gospel of Matthew tries to soften the crassness of the brothers' request in Mark by having the *mother* of James and John ask Jesus for the distinguished positions of power in his coming kingdom (Matt 20:20).

We come now to Acts. Sure enough, John is present in the early chapters alongside Peter. There are actually three Johns mentioned in Acts: John

A Complicated Love Story

the Baptizer, John the son of Zebedee and brother of James, and John Mark. The particular John with whom we are interested is the son of Zebedee. He appears early in Acts alongside Peter. The two men were going to the temple of Jerusalem at three o'clock in the afternoon, the time of prayer. They met a man lame from birth. He was begging alms at the Beautiful Gate of the temple. The lame man asked alms from Peter and John. Peter alone responded: "I have no silver or gold, but what I have I give you; in the name of Jesus Christ of Nazareth, stand up and walk" (Acts 3:6). The man stood up and walked, and the people were amazed at the miracle, at which point Peter alone delivered a mini sermon about the grace and power of God in the person of Jesus (Acts 3:11–13). The two apostles then went to Samaria together to bear witness to Jesus there. Their ministry in Samaria complete, both Peter and John returned to Jerusalem, and John the son of Zebedee thereafter vanishes from the rest of the long story in Acts.

This much is evident from this little foray into three significant sources. John was *not* a major player alongside the Peter. He was a minor figure in Galatians, last on the list of three leaders; in the Synoptic Gospels he and his brother wanted Jesus to enable them to call down fire from heaven to kill Samaritans; they also asked Jesus for prestigious seats in the coming kingdom; Peter and John appear together in Acts, but it is Peter alone who heals a lame man, and delivers sermons. John is completely silent in Acts and heals no one.

(2) As noted above, the person and name of John appears only once in all of Paul's letters, and that insignificantly. To be sure, John the son of Zebedee was included in the list of three "pillars" guiding the new Jewish Christian community in Jerusalem. But John certainly was not a leader with whom Paul debated, or one to whom he had to give account. By contrast, Peter traveled to the mission field where Paul was gathering in gentile converts, particularly at Antioch. Paul ended up estranged from Peter because he withdrew from eating non-kosher food with uncircumcised gentiles. Peter's withdrawal from Paul happened when some people appeared in Antioch, having come from James the brother of Jesus in Jerusalem (Gal 2:11–14). That rift between Peter and Paul was never fully repaired. The important point to be made here, in keeping with our quest, is that Peter was not answerable to John, but to James of Jerusalem, the brother of Jesus. Nor was Peter dependent on John to guide his thinking or his steps. In short, the persons of Peter and John in the letters of Paul do not square with Peter and the Beloved Disciple in the Fourth Gospel. The disciple Jesus loved,

according to the Fourth Gospel, outperforms Peter in every way, connects Peter with Jesus during the meal, and even runs faster than Peter to the empty tomb.

Turning now to the Synoptic Gospels, what do we find there concerning John, son of Zebedee? It's important not to get the Johns of the Synoptic Gospels mixed up. John the Baptizer is highly honored in those Gospels, but John the Baptizer was not the son of Zebedee. Here is Jesus's verdict concerning John the Baptizer: "among those born of women no one has arisen greater than John the Baptist" (Matt 11:11; Luke 7:28). Nothing of the sort is said of John the son of Zebedee. The identity of John in the Synoptics is signaled simply as "the brother of James" (Matt 4:21; 10:2; Mark 3:17; 5:37). Unlike the towering figure of the disciple whom Jesus loved in the Book of the Passion, John in the Synoptic Gospels is frequently found in third place in a list of disciples, whereas in the Book of the Passion the beloved disciple is consistently highlighted as the significant one among the others. There is one place in Luke where Jesus gives both Peter and John an important job to do for him: "Jesus sent Peter and John, saying, 'Go and prepare the Passover meal for us that we may eat it'" (Luke 22:8). But even here, John is in second position next to Peter in the twosome, quite the opposite to what we find in the Book of the Passion in the Fourth Gospel with respect to the disciple whom Jesus loved. That disciple outperforms Peter in the Fourth Gospel and is therefore in the dominant position.

What of Acts? The same situation exists. To be sure, John is present with Peter, but that's about all that can be said of him. Peter is the spokesperson and the healer of the lame man. John is merely alongside, and speechless in Acts. This much is evident: Peter is the more dominant figure of the twosome. He is consistently cited in first position and John in second: "Peter and John." This positioning in Acts is consistent and frequent (ten times in all). Not once is it reversed. To my mind, this consistent positioning of the two names at key junctures in Acts implies that John bows to the leadership of Peter.

With this evidence from the three sources in mind, one is hard-pressed to identify John, son of Zebedee, as the outstanding character of the beloved disciple in the Book of the Passion in the Fourth Gospel. In that setting Peter bows to the leadership of the beloved disciple, and especially to his *special* relationship with Jesus. Now comes the test. If the special disciple in the Fourth Gospel were *not* John, son of Zebedee, then who might he be? Why would Jesus love him above all the others? Answers to these questions should follow three indisputable propositions concerning the disciple that Jesus loved as evidenced in the Book of the Passion in the Fourth Gospel: (1) He would need to have a very special relationship with Jesus to warrant the distinctive designation, "the disciple that Jesus loved." (2) He would have to possess leadership skills and trustworthiness beyond those of Peter. (3) He would require a right spirit and a special relationship with the mother of Jesus to take responsibility for her welfare in his own home following Jesus's death. There may be more, but these three will suffice to make the case for this one disciple that Jesus loved: *his brother, James.*

What follows is a weaving together of material from two principal sources within the New Testament to make the case: two letters of Paul and the book of Acts. The first item to remember is that Jesus had more than twelve disciples. The Gospel of Luke tells of seventy in addition to the twelve (Luke 10:1, 17). Other disciples beyond these two symbolic groups doubtless believed in Jesus and followed his life and ministry. In order to become a leading figure in the community of Jewish believers in Jesus in Jerusalem following the death and resurrection of Jesus one would be expected to know his mind and his teaching. What I hope to demonstrate is that James the brother of Jesus is the most likely candidate.

According to some non-biblical sources, this disciple earned the honorific title, "James the Just," i.e. "the righteous one." If this James had not been a close follower of Jesus, and very well-known to Jesus during his public ministry, his rise to such an influential position in the early church in Jerusalem would be an anomaly. His principal leadership in the Christian community of Jerusalem is borne out in the letters of Paul and also in the book of Acts. And as noted above, other non-biblical documents, too numerous to explore here, complement those of the New Testament.[6]

Our focus here will be on the two sources in the New Testament. The earliest and clearest reference to the principal leadership of James the brother of Jesus in Jerusalem appears in two letters of Paul. In 1 Cor 15:7 Paul affirms that the risen Jesus "appeared to James, then to all the apostles." I think it is significant that James is singled out here as worthy of particular recognition from among "all the apostles." It needs to be said boldly: this James was the brother of Jesus, second oldest son in the family of Mary and Joseph, according to Mark 6:3 (cf. Matt 13:55). But this brother of Jesus comes even more to the forefront in Paul's letter to the Galatians.

---

6. See my chapter, "Legendary James the Just," 121–50.

In Gal 1:19 Paul notes that when he went up to Jerusalem three years after his encounter with the risen Jesus he met up with Peter, and "did not see any other apostle *except James the Lord's brother.*" So James is here clearly acknowledged as brother of Jesus, and also his apostle. (By inference from silence Paul did not see John son of Zebedee on that trip). Paul wrote this piece of information in the mid-50s of the first century, but dates the event happening three years after his encounter with the risen Jesus, and his foray "at once" into Arabia. So his meeting with Peter and James in Jerusalem on that occasion may be dated at ca. 35 CE. In Gal 2 Paul continues his personal history about meeting the three leaders in Jerusalem. "After fourteen years I went up again to Jerusalem with Barnabas, taking Titus along with me ... Then I laid before them (though only in a private meeting with the acknowledged leaders) the gospel that I proclaim among the Gentiles, in order to make sure that I was not running, or had not run, in vain." Paul recognized the need to link his mission to gentiles with the primary Jewish community of Jesus Messiah in Jerusalem. He did so by meeting with the three recognized leaders of the parent community: "James and [Peter] and John." Paul's radical mission to gentiles could easily have threatened the long-standing Jewish identity, which Jesus upheld in his mission in Palestine. Paul, on the other hand, had set aside *three key marks* of Jewish identity to allow gentiles entrance into the spirit of Jesus Messiah: circumcision, kosher food, and seventh-day Sabbath observance.

Paul recalls "when James and [Peter] and John ... recognized the grace that had been given to me, they gave to Barnabas and me the right hand of fellowship, agreeing that we should go to the Gentiles and they to the circumcised" (Gal 2:9). It is hard to shed longstanding identity, whether genetic, biographical, religious, or communal. And hard also to have "outsiders" lay claim to the good grace of that identity while ignoring some of its treasured symbols. So Peter headed north from Jerusalem to Antioch to check out the mission situation in which Paul was engaged. He went along with Paul's open table fellowship; even joined Paul and his gentile converts at the table, "until certain people came from James" of Jerusalem (Gal 2:12). Peter ultimately honored the status of James, and withdrew from Paul, taking Barnabas and others with him. Paul says he "opposed [Peter] to his face, because he stood self-condemned; for until certain people came from James, he used to eat with the Gentiles" (Gal 2:11–12). I suspect James believed he was honoring the mission of his brother, Jesus, who stayed well within the bounds of the traditional land of ancient Israel on the one hand,

and within the law of Moses on the other. Consider, for example, Jesus's encounter with a non-Jewish Syrophoenician woman who wanted him to heal her child. According to Matthew, "he did not answer her at all." But he spoke, it seems, to his disciples, saying: "I was sent only to the lost sheep of the house of Israel." And to the woman he said: "It is not fair to take the children's food and throw it to the dogs" (Matt 15:22–26; cf. Mark 7:25–29). James probably knew something of this strongly Jewish orientation in the ministry of his brother Jesus. If so, he may have had theological qualms about mixing devoutly observant Jewish Christians with not-so-observant gentile Christians. The non-Palestinian Paul, on the other hand, may have found it easier to accommodate the gentiles than the devoutly Jewish Palestinian James, brother of Jesus.

Time now to turn the spotlight on the book of Acts for another angle on James the Just and Peter his partner in relation to Paul and his gentile world mission. As I intimated in an earlier chapter, Acts 1 puts the mother of Jesus together with his brothers at prayer in an upstairs room in Jerusalem following Jesus's death and resurrection. They were there along with the twelve disciples to await direction for the future of the movement that Jesus had initiated before his death. Our interest here is specifically with James the brother of Jesus. Is he present in the account in Acts? Is he a leading figure in Acts with Peter by his side? The answer is unequivocally yes. Let me explain.

There were many people called "James" in Jewish Jerusalem of the time. Several of them appear in Acts, including James the brother of John who met his death tragically at the hands of Herod, grandson of Herod the Great (Acts 12:2). Also mentioned in Acts is James the son of Alphaeus, and Judas son of James (Acts 1:13). Beyond these three there is only James the son of Joseph and Mary, even though his family connection is not given in Acts. The name "James" comes from the Hebrew name "Jacob." That highly respected name lies behind every occurrence of "James" in the New Testament. No wonder it became a common name in Jewish Palestine. Jacob was the father-founder of the nation of Israel. So common was the name "James" in the first century it usually required an additional qualifier, as in James the son of Alphaeus. Oddly enough James the brother of Jesus stands out in Acts by the *absence* of any family identity. Yet we know very well from Paul's letter to the Galatians that James the brother of Jesus was the chief leader of the Jewish community of Jesus Messiah in Jerusalem, and that Peter was his coworker.

The Beloved Disciple in the Spotlight

Herod, who had James killed, also imprisoned Peter, intending to take his life as well. While Peter was in prison a miracle happened. Peter's chains loosed, the prison door opened, and Peter walked away. He made his way to the house of Mary, John Mark's mother. The people inside were astonished to see him. After a few comments about his prison experience, Peter promptly instructed someone thus: "Tell this to James and to the believers" (Acts 12:12–17). This James is none other than the brother of Jesus, who was not imprisoned, presumably because he had a good connection with the temple hierarchy. But here is something very strange. The translators of the NRSV mistranslated one very important word in Peter's instruction. Literally, the instruction reads: "Tell these things to James and *the brothers*" (Gk. *adelphoi*). I do not know for sure the motivation behind the mistranslation of *adelphoi*, "brothers," except that the translators probably wanted inclusive language. But that would constitute a misreading of the text in context. This particular case is about James and his *biological* brothers, as in Acts 1:14. On that occasion the *brothers* of Jesus had gathered in the upstairs room in Jerusalem awaiting further wisdom on how to proceed. James, as we know, was the leading brother among the others, the one next in age to Jesus: the same James we met in Paul's letters, and will meet again later on in Acts (Mark 6:3; 1 Cor 9:5).

There are two other places in Acts where James the brother of Jesus comes into focus. One is in Acts 15 where the charter of Paul's mission to gentiles comes under close scrutiny. As noted earlier, Paul had declared some of the longstanding requirements for entrance in covenantal Judaism no longer applicable to gentiles since the death and resurrection of Jesus Messiah. Moreover, Paul granted his gentile converts equal status in that new covenant with the same standing as Jewish Christians in Jerusalem. From the perspective of Jewish Christianity in Jerusalem, however, such a practice constituted a breach of trust in the "everlasting covenant" Yahweh/God made with his people (Gen 17:13). Here is an example of the response from one group of conservative Jewish believers in Jesus Messiah. "But some believers who belonged to the sect of the Pharisees stood up and said, 'It is necessary for them [Gentiles] to be circumcised and ordered to keep the law of Moses'" (Acts 15:5). Circumcision of adult males was the real litmus test of genuine transfer into the covenant God made with Moses. Paul must have witnessed the reaction of the male gentiles especially to the idea of circumcision, and decided that the outward marks, whether circumcision, kosher, or Sabbath, could be rendered inoperative in the presence of the Sprit of Jesus in the community of faith. At any rate, that was the debate between Paul and the two key leaders of the Jerusalem-Jewish side, James and Peter.

According to Acts, Peter spoke to the issue first, concluding that God, "in cleansing their [Gentiles] hearts by faith he has made no distinction between them and us.... On the contrary, we believe that we will be saved through the grace of the Lord Jesus, just as they will" (Acts 15:9, 11). Paul and Barnabas then speak a few words along the same line. Then comes James, the brother of Jesus, with the binding word and action on the matter. Here is part of his speech in Acts 15:14–21.

> My brothers, listen to me. Simeon [Peter] has related how God first looked favorably on the Gentiles, to take from among them a people for his name. This agrees with the words of the prophets.... Therefore I have reached the decision that we should not trouble those Gentiles who are turning to God, but we should write to them to abstain only from things polluted by idols and from fornication and from whatever has been strangled and from blood. For in every city, for generations past, Moses has had those who proclaim him, for he has been read aloud every sabbath in the synagogues.

It was James, not Peter, who brought the matter to a close, made the decision, wrote the letter, and dispatched it to gentile believers in Antioch and Syria. Thus, here in Acts, written so many years after the events, James is remembered as the leading figure among the apostles of Jesus. He is clearly the principal leader of the church in Jerusalem, to whom Peter is obliged to give account, and to whom also Paul and Barnabas are obliged to report. This brave disciple-apostle, James, is the brother of Jesus, the disciple whom Jesus loved in a special brotherly way, and the one whom Peter is obliged to respect, as evident in Acts 15.

One final foray into Acts will bring this part of the chapter to a close. This time the spotlight falls on Paul and James in Jerusalem, reported in Acts 21. After his active and successful mission among the gentiles in Asia Minor, Macedonia, and Greece, Paul decided to visit Jerusalem with an offering of money from the gentile congregations to the "saints" in Jerusalem (Rom 15:23–27). It seems he wanted to clear his name and his mission once and for all before going west to Rome and beyond. His questionable reputation preceded him in Jerusalem, so his reception in the Holy City was less than hospitable. On his way to the hub of the city to deliver the money and speak to the Jewish authorities about his work, Paul decided to visit with the most notable apostle. That apostle was *not* Peter. In fact, Peter's name does not occur in Acts after chapter 15. The notable apostle to whom Paul presented himself was James, the brother of Jesus. The narrative is often referred to as belonging to the "we" section of Acts. No one knows for sure what the "we" represents. Nor does it matter. I think it behooves us, however, to read a significant portion of the text in Acts 21 to understand Paul's situation, and no less that of James the Just, brother of Jesus. I have highlighted key terms and phrases to ponder. I shall address them briefly following the text in Acts.

> When we arrived in Jerusalem, the *brothers* welcomed us warmly. The next day Paul went with us to visit *James*; and all the elders were present. After greeting them, he [Paul] related one by one the things that God had done among the Gentiles through his ministry. When they heard it, they praised God. Then they said to him, "You see, brother, how many thousands of believers there are among the Jews, and they are all zealous for *the law*. They have been told about you that you teach *all the Jews* living among the Gentiles to forsake Moses, and that you tell them not to circumcise their children or observe the customs. What then is to be done? They will certainly hear that you have come. So do what we tell you. We have four men who are under a vow. Join these men, go through the rite of *purification* with them, and pay for the shaving of their heads. Thus all will know that there is nothing in what they have been told about you, but that you yourself observe and guard the law. But as for the Gentiles who have become believers, we have sent *a letter* with our judgment that they should abstain from what has been sacrificed to idols and from blood and from what is strangled and from fornication." (Acts 21:17–25)

It is interesting, if not a little strange, to find the NRSV scholars translating the Greek word *adelphoi* this time as *brothers*. Previously in Acts 12, as we saw, the translation of the same word was "believers." It is possible that "the brothers" here also refers to the brothers of Jesus, with James the leading brother. After visiting the brothers upon arrival in Jerusalem, Paul went the next day to visit *James* alone. It seems to me quite plausible that the whole family of Jesus lived in Jerusalem following the death and resurrecting of Jesus (Acts 1:14).

James is doubtless the same James we met in chapters 12 and 15 of Acts. He is the eldest of the brothers of Jesus, and as such highly regarded for his leadership of the family and the larger church in Jerusalem (Mark 6).

A Complicated Love Story

The law continues to be an issue for Paul as he meets with his Jewish Christian counterparts in Jerusalem. The argument of the Jewish believers in Jesus in Jerusalem seems to be that the law of God was given for a good purpose. A true believer does not pick and choose which parts to obey and which parts to disregard. That seems to be the argument of the Jewish Christians in Jerusalem, against Paul's practice among gentiles.

It seems there was also misinformation circulating in Jerusalem. There is no indication in Paul's correspondence that he was teaching *all the Jews* to forsake Moses, nor that he told Jews not to circumcise their male infants.

In Judaism, *purification* rituals were very much a part of observing the law of Moses. Paul's friends in the home of James of Jerusalem urged him to go through the rite of purification along with other men, and pay for the shaving of their heads. In that way he might be seen as observing the law.

The *letter* referred to here is the same one cited in Acts 15. James was the writer of the message. Oddly enough the instruction in the letter to Paul's Christ-following communities is silent on the question of circumcision of males, kosher food guidelines, and Sabbath keeping. Paul required none of these major marks of Jewish identity from his gentile believers.

From where I sit, two of the three leading propositions relative to the disciple that Jesus loved have been demonstrated: (1) He would need to have a very special relationship with Jesus to warrant the distinctive designation, "the disciple that Jesus loved." James the brother Jesus meets the criteria better than any other disciple of Jesus, including especially John the son of Zebedee. (2) He would have to possess leadership skills and trustworthiness beyond those of Peter. The testimony from Paul's letters and from Acts points to brother James, not to John the son of Zebedee. Now the third and final proposition lies before us ready for the test: (3) He would require a compassionate spirit and a special relationship with the mother of Jesus to accept responsibility for her welfare in his own home following Jesus's death.

Recall from an earlier chapter that Jesus passed the responsibility of his mother to the disciple he loved. And that person took her to *his own home* from that day forward. What I did not mention in that earlier chapter was the likely identity of the disciple who accepted the responsibility, nor did I suggest the location of the disciple's home where the mother of Jesus was expected to live. Those two important pieces of the puzzle must now be tested in the context of what we have discovered already.

The Beloved Disciple in the Spotlight

Before doing so, let me begin with a true short story to illustrate what we are up against. I was slated to speak in a church in western Canada. When I arrived rather early in the sanctuary one of the assistant pastors wanted to talk to me about the Fourth Gospel. The pastor repeatedly made reference to "John" when referring to the beloved disciple. I stopped him, and asked why he kept using the name "John" when the Fourth Gospel does not provide such a name. The pastor was puzzled. "Why would you ask that?" he inquired. "Everyone knows John was the disciple Jesus loved." I responded as follows: "I ask it because there is no one named John in any of the texts you have cited. In fact the person of John the son of Zebedee does not appear anywhere within the Fourth Gospel." More puzzled still, he said, "Well at least John was standing at the foot of the cross when Jesus transferred responsibility of his mother to him." I had to point out again that even in that place John is nowhere in the passion narrative of the Fourth Gospel, least of all at the foot of the cross where some male figure is asked to take responsibility for the mother of Jesus. This true story is meant to alert all of us, myself included, to the extraordinary power of untested churchly tradition to overshadow, or overpower, evidence within the text of Scripture itself.

It should go without saying, having explored the relevant sources in the New Testament, that *the least compelling male character* standing at the foot of the cross of Jesus would be John the son of Zebedee. Since Peter is not listed as present at the foot of the cross, then rest assured John the son of Zebedee would not be present. But more to the point, why in the world would Jesus commit the care of his mother to a disciple totally unrelated to his mother? It makes no sense at all. Furthermore, what would such a transfer of responsibility to a non-relative signal concerning the other sons of the mother of Jesus? Were her sons all renegades, unworthy of such responsibility? We know better than that by now. We have found the brothers with their mother in the upstairs room awaiting direction from the Spirit about moving forward with the message of Jesus Messiah. And we have met the brother next to Jesus, James, heavily involved in creating a community of faith in Jesus Messiah. It would be a most serious insult for Jesus to transfer responsibility for his mother to a nonrelative when such a worthy son as James would do right by his mother.

The fact is there is only one male figure standing at the foot of the cross together with some women including the mother of Jesus. "When Jesus saw his mother and the disciple whom he loved standing beside her, he said to his mother, 'Woman, here is your son.' Then he said to the disciple, 'Here is your mother.' And from that hour the disciple took her into his own home" (19:26–27). There is not a hint here that the anonymous disciple later took Mary away from Jerusalem to another place entirely, many miles away in a Greek environment. That raises the question of the location of the home where Mary spent the last years of her life.[7]

Tradition purports that the apostle John built a house for Mary in the vicinity of Ephesus. I visited the house in 1995, and found numerous people paying homage to the "Blessed Virgin" believed to have lived there. But I was not at all convinced then or now that the tradition is historically sound. I strongly believe that the last place the mother of Jesus would feel at home would be in or near Ephesus, a Greek city in what is today Turkey. Yet that "House of Mary" near the bustling city of Ephesus is now endorsed by the Catholic Church as the house of the Virgin Mary, based largely on the visions of a nineteenth-century nun, Blessed Anne Catherine Emmerich (1774–1824 CE). Keep in mind, the mother of Jesus raised her family in ancient Palestine, worshiped Yahweh/God at the temple of Jerusalem, and lived as a *Jewish* woman of faith among *Jewish* women. I cannot imagine how she would have felt in a Greek environment such as Ephesus. But the tradition insists that Mary left behind her familiar territory in Palestine, including her family of sons and daughters (Mark 6:3). She is said to have followed a non-family disciple of Jesus into a strongly Hellenistic environment, namely Ephesus, approximately 1,850 kilometers from Jerusalem. (Having walked through the ancient ruins of Ephesus, I can attest to its largely non-Jewish character from the cultural remains I observed).

Now let's consider the more likely scenario, based on the evidence from the New Testament. James the brother of Jesus lived in Jerusalem after Jesus's death. That much we have demonstrated unequivocally from the letters of Paul and the book of Acts. To suggest that the mother of Jesus would be better off with John the son of Zebedee in the city of Ephesus would be downright irresponsible. And implicitly to characterize James the son of Mary and brother of Jesus as a self-centered son who would not care for his mother would be completely out of character for James. He was a devout Jew who engaged in the service of the temple; he was also a follower of his beloved brother Jesus who was likewise Jewish. To suggest that Jesus would not commit the care of his mother to her own son, James of Jerusalem, lacks credibility. The supporting evidence I have adduced from the relevant

---

7. Brown, *Life of Mary*, 209–16.

New Testament texts is irrefutable. James earned the title "James the Just." Righteous man that he was, he took responsibility for his beloved mother after Jesus's death. The lesson is this: tradition should not be allowed to trump reasonable evidence drawn from reliable and relevant sources.

One question remains unanswered: Why did the writer of the Fourth Gospel cloak this worthy disciple of Jesus in total anonymity? No one really knows the final answer for sure. What I am about to give here in conclusion to this chapter is my best guess.

Recall the lateness of the writing of this Fourth Gospel, compared, let's say, to the letters of Paul. Social, political, and religious factors operating at the time of writing, especially in ancient societies, really do influence how the internal discourse is set forth. By the time the Fourth Gospel was written the *Jewish* Christian community was slowly but surely diminishing while the gentile world mission was forging ahead. As noted above, the devout James of Jerusalem, who prayed daily in the temple, also sought diligently to foster a right spirit within the Jewish-Christian communities in the city. The Roman prefect who came to power surreptitiously took serious umbrage against James the Just to the point of ordering his death by stoning. James died as a result in ca. 62 CE. The Jewish Christian community in Jerusalem over which he presided was shattered by the loss of their precious leader. The groups continued to gather for worship in Jerusalem until the war broke out in 66 CE. The fledgling community over which James had presided feared for their lives.

Consequently, they made their way to Jordan, east of the river and south of the territory of Galilee. The community slowly but surely lost its identity as the community of Jesus Messiah over which James had presided successfully until his death. As time went by the Jordan community of Jesus Messiah disappeared from the Jewish Christian landscape altogether. It became a memory merely, one that the author of the Fourth Gospel chose not to tarnish by bringing its beloved leader, James the Just, brother of Jesus, into sharp focus in the Book of the Passion. A failed entity rarely figures prominently in the annals of history. The author of the Fourth Gospel, knowing about the good work of James the Just, brother of Jesus, chose to honor his memory as the worthy brother-disciple that Jesus loved without divulging his given name. Jesus loved him as he loved all his disciples, but loved him also on the level of a biological brother. Hence his uniqueness as the disciple that Jesus loved. The two of them played together as boys in Nazareth. They ate from the same food at the same table growing up.

They attended the same synagogue services. They learned to work alongside their father and mother. Their life together in Palestine spanned some twenty-five years. This puts Jesus's special love-relationship with James a good notch above that of any other disciple.

I cannot find a more compelling response than what I have given above to the implied question arising out of the Book of the Passion in the Fourth Gospel: What would have motivated Jesus to love one disciple above and beyond his love for all the other disciples?

12

Pontius Pilate and the Question of Truth

THE CONTEXT OF PILATE's loaded question to Jesus should help us glimpse his character in asking as he did: "What is truth?" (18:38). It was a provocative question, then as now. The genuineness of his inquiry is debatable. Before attempting to deal with that otherwise valid and profound question about truth, I think it worthwhile to discuss the historical person of Pontius Pilate: his background, political position at the time of Jesus, character and behavior depicted in the four Gospels, and character and behavior from sources other than the four Gospels.

BACKGROUND

Pilate's full name was Marcus Pontius Pilatus. His date of birth is not on record, so we are left with the adult man and his place within the politics of imperial Rome. It is generally believed that he was born in a village in central Italy, and made his way into Roman politics at a relatively young age. He served as prefect, or governor, of Judea for ten years, 26–36 CE. Emperor Tiberius appointed him to that post. He was the fifth prefect to occupy the position in Judea. While there is not abundant textual evidence of Pilate's career as prefect of Judea, there is one significant piece of hard evidence known as the Pilate Stone. Archaeologists discovered the reused block of limestone in 1961 in the vicinity of the Roman theater at Caesarea-by-the-sea, the administrative hub of the province of Judea at the time. The inscription on the stone gives Pilate's name, and is dated within the timeframe of his rule in Judea. I first saw the inscribed stone on location at Caesarea when I was in Israel in 1977. The stone was later moved to the Israel Museum.

POLITICAL POSITION

Pilate set up his headquarters in the maritime city of Caesarea. Much seafaring traffic docked in the port, and brought into the city all kinds of goods from different parts of the Mediterranean world. But Pilate was not an independent ruler of the state of Judea. He was forever answerable to Emperor Tiberius in Rome. And more than once the Jewish citizens lodged complaints about undeserved harsh treatment from Pilate. Tiberius Caesar brought him to heel rather than let him generate a political uprising in Judea. Pilate's principal job in the region was to act as guardian of *Pax Romana*, "Roman Peace." His character was scarcely suited to the job, as we shall see momentarily. Imperial Rome was forever on guard against treason. If such treason were found within the Judean community it was swiftly punished, often by execution in the form of crucifixion. And Pilate was regularly on the lookout for any sign of treason among the Jewish people. Kingship in Judea had effectively disappeared, to be replaced by the rule of the caesar/king of the Roman Empire through minions such as Pilate. Tiberius Caesar gave Pilate quite a bit of latitude in determining treason worthy of death.

CHARACTER AND BEHAVIOR IN THE GOSPELS

Pilate's name and rule of order appears prominently in all four Gospels of the New Testament, also in Acts (3:13; 4:27; 13:28), and marginally in 1 Timothy (6:13). He comes across in the Gospel literature and Acts as a conciliatory figure, unwilling to go along with the Jewish leaders' judgment of Jesus as antagonistic to Rome, and thereby worthy of execution. Pilate appears in the Gospels as a sympathetic ruler eager to set Jesus free. This posture in the Gospels is hard to fathom, given Pilate's reputation elsewhere as a ruthless bully. In the Gospel of Matthew, for example, Pilate washes his hands as a sign to the Jewish leaders that he would not bear responsibility for the conviction and death of Jesus (Matt 27:24). The Gospel of Mark is not quite as pro-Pilate as the other Gospels. Pilate does debate with the Jewish judges about the culpability of Jesus. He asks the accusers what evil Jesus has done to deserve execution. Then he releases a criminal, Barabbas, to them instead, and has Jesus flogged and ultimately crucified (Mark 15:14).

The Gospel of Luke is the most pro-Roman of all the Gospels. At one point in Luke, members of the Sanhedrin told Pilate that Jesus tried to persuade the Jews not to pay taxes to Rome (Luke 23:2). While there is not much evidence to this effect, there is some. Jesus had asked Levi to leave his booth where he collected taxes for Rome (Mark 2:14). Zacchaeus also appears to have abandoned his job as tax collector (Luke 19:2–8). With the case building against Jesus, Luke's Pilate is unable to release him, even though he can find no fault in him (Luke 23:20). Pilate even summoned Herod Antipas of Galilee to interrogate Jesus, and hopefully save him from execution. Jesus had lived under Herod's rule in Galilee and did not suffer sanction from him. Herod, like Pilate, is not able to find anything in Jesus worthy of death (Luke 23:15). So Luke places virtually all of the blame for the crucifixion of Jesus on the Jewish Sanhedrin.

A similar version comes through in the Fourth Gospel. Pilate is the relatively good guy who finds no fault in Jesus, against the urging of the Jewish leaders who want Pilate to crucify him (18:31). Members of the Sanhedrin say they are not permitted to put anyone to death, so Pilate has to do the deed for them. Pilate then asks Jesus the highly charged political question: "Are you the king of the Jews?" (18:33). That loaded question lies at the heart of the matter. Jesus gives a carefully qualified answer, without denying that he is a king: "My kingdom is not from this world. If my kingdom were from this world, my followers would be fighting to keep me from being handed over to the Jews. But as it is, my kingdom is not from here" (18:36). Pilate responds: "So you are a king?" (18:37). Then Jesus answers unequivocally: "You say that I am a king. For this I was born, and for this I came into the world, to testify to the truth. Everyone who belongs to the truth listens to my voice" (18:37). The words "king" and "kingdom," however well qualified, were politically hot topics in that time and place. No one in the Roman Empire could make such claims without serious judgment from the political representative of imperial Rome. The Jewish leaders knew the rule of Rome on the matter of kingship, so they tried to stomp out the slightest whiff of the topic of kingship from their people for the sake of peace and security in Judea.

A Complicated Love Story

CHARACTER AND BEHAVIOR FROM OTHER SOURCES

Quite another image of Pontius Pilate develops from sources other than the four Gospels of the New Testament. Two sources written in the first century will serve to illustrate. Both writers were respected Jewish scholars. Both of them paint a rather bleak picture of Pilate: Philo in Egypt, and Josephus of Palestine.

Philo (20 BCE–50 CE) was a well-educated Jew who lived in the city of Alexandria in Egypt. He spoke and wrote in Greek, out of a broad knowledge of the Greco-Roman world in which he lived. I shall give a brief sampling of his testimony to the character of Pilate. According to Philo, Emperor Tiberius reproved Pilate for antagonizing the Jews. Apparently he installed gold shields in Herod's palace in Jerusalem as a symbol of honor to the emperor, and thus he raised the ire of the Jews against Tiberius. Jewish leaders reported Pilate to Tiberius. Philo also wrote about Pilate's temper and his self-centeredness. He describes him variously as corrupt, insulting, cruel, and murderous. This description scarcely resembles the portrait of Pilate in the four Gospels of the New Testament.[8]

Josephus (37 CE–100 CE) paints a similar picture of Pilate during his tenure as prefect of Judea. He disrespected Jewish customs, especially their law concerning idols. According to Josephus, Pilate instructed his soldiers to bring various images and effigies representative of Caesar into Jerusalem at night. When the Jewish leaders saw the images next morning, they begged Pilate to have them removed. He refused. Pilate's soldiers stood guard over the images, while keeping the Jewish demonstrators at bay. That appeal to Pilate lasted five days. Instead of listening to the Jewish people, Pilate threatened them with death if they persisted on their course. He seemed unaware of the Jews' profound commitment to their law. They would willingly die rather than yield to such a violation of the law of Moses, which prohibited the worship of images or idols. In the end, Pilate was obliged to remove the images. His appointed position in Judea was at stake. This critical description of Pilate does not square with what we find in the four Gospels of New Testament.[9]

It is not easy to account for the different pictures between the rather positive image of Pilate in the four Gospels and the more negative

---

8. Philo, *Legat.*
9. Josephus, *Ant.* 18:35–177; Josephus, *War* 2:169–75.

Pontius Pilate and the Question of Truth

description of him from two respected Jewish writers from the same period. Neither of them witnessed the trial of Jesus in Jerusalem. But Josephus exhibits knowledge of the trial and execution of Jesus over which Pilate presided. The information was gleaned, presumably, from contemporary members of the Christian community living at the latter end of the first century.[10]

What follows here echoes what other scholars have put forward variously in their attempts to understand the seemingly irreconcilable difference between the accounts in the four Gospels and Acts, and those of Philo and Josephus.

When the four Gospels were written the community of Jesus Messiah had already taken hold inside and outside Palestine, more so outside. The growth of the new community of Jesus happened especially among the gentiles following the launching of the gentile world mission. The non-messianic Jews increasingly distanced themselves from the new messianic movement under the name of Jesus of Nazareth, a movement that had become increasingly gentile. Enmity grew between the two communities. So the Gospels accordingly cast the otherwise-harsh Pilate of Rome in a somewhat sympathetic manner in tension with the Jewish Sanhedrin. Leaders in the Sanhedrin wanted Pilate to crucify Jesus; Pilate tries to dissuade them. He finally is forced to yield to their decision to sentence Jesus to death by crucifixion, making the Jewish Sanhedrin the truly guilty party, and Pilate not so much. The rendering of the court proceedings in the four Gospels probably grew out of the tension between the synagogue and the church in the post-Temple period. But as we shall discover in the next chapter, the powerful Pilate was in fact the one to sentence Jesus to death by crucifixion with unwavering determination, as the Fourth Evangelist is ultimately obliged to concede.

WHAT IS TRUTH?

"What is Truth? said jesting Pilate; and would not stay for an answer." That is Francis Bacon's opening line to his essay, "Of Truth" (ca. 1597). It echoes the text of 18:38b in the Fourth Gospel: "After [Pilate] had said this, he went out to the Jews again." The impression is that Pilate was not really interested in an answer to his question about truth.

10. Josephus, *Ant.* 18:62–64.

A Complicated Love Story

Truth (*alêtheia*) is one of the major themes in the Fourth Gospel. The subject needs to be explored carefully beyond what I am prepared to do here. It would be an interesting question for a small group to discuss: "What is truth?" The answer may seem obvious at first glance. But the more one ponders the ramifications of the question the greater the need for some serious study. The truth may be hard to handle at times, but the alternative surely leads to chaos. I shall first highlight a few of the more striking images occurring in the Fourth Gospel, followed by a brief discussion of the *necessity* of truth and truth-telling for understanding ourselves in society and culture and religion, and also in relation to the universe in which we live.

In the voice of the narrator:

- 1:14: The incarnate *logos*-son was "full of grace and *truth*."

In the voice of Jesus:

- 4:24: "Those who worship [God] must worship in spirit and *truth*."
- 8:32: "You will know the *truth* and the *truth* will make you free."
- 14:6: "I am the way, and the *truth*, and the life."
- 17:17: "Sanctify [the disciples] in the *truth*; your word is *truth*."
- 18:37: "I came into the world, to testify to the *truth*."

Simply put, truth is that which corresponds to reality. Usually we view truth in terms of human speech. In human community we expect truth to be the norm for worthwhile exchange of ideas and directives in business, family, and politics. Knowing the truth and telling the truth to each other in society is not an option. It is a necessity. Otherwise society crashes to the ground. But there is more to truth than telling. We need to understand clearly that truth and human reason are compatible partners. Animals do not speak and act as human beings do. Animals are not capable of reasoning, and are therefore not held responsible for committing falsehood. Instinct and training are the rule for animals, not human language and not reason. Human beings are capable of generating situations that do *not* correspond to reality, and are thereby *not* following truth. If the falsehood is made known as such then the "falsehood" becomes an aspect of truth.

Jesus, according to the Synoptic Gospels, spoke in parables to challenge his audience to think outside the box of everyday reality. The provocative parable generated a fresh image in the minds of Jesus's audience. But the parable was not true in the usual sense of truth corresponding to reality. The generated parable story of Jesus pushed the audience to question the validity of their adopted situation in the society of the time.

The best example would be the parable of the Samaritan who stopped to bind up the wounds of the human victim of abuse (Luke 10:25–37). The story was told to a Jewish audience. The listeners would assume that the victim on the side of the road was a Jew, not a Samaritan, "for the Jews have no dealings with the Samaritans" (4:9 KJV). When the super-generous Samaritan appears in the parable, after the two Jewish neighbors have passed by the suffering Jew on the side of the road, the Jewish audience would wince at the very idea. So the contrived parable of Jesus had the effect of jolting the Jewish listeners into rethinking their attitude towards the human neighbor, regardless of their gender, race, religion, or social status. The point is that the story Jesus told, while not true to life at the time, was understood as "parable," i.e. a story thrown alongside the truth to affect change for good.

Truth, in its various guises, sets people free from deceit and constriction and loss. Let me illustrate with a true story coming from my native homeland of Ireland. A number of years ago a farmer in Ireland, since deceased, found it necessary to sell his farm. It was time to retire. He hoped to secure enough funds from the sale of the farm to provide for his wife and himself with food and shelter for the rest of their lives. The farm had a right-of-way running through it. The farmer decided not to reveal that piece of information to the prospective buyer. He would tell the truth about everything else, and simply remain silent about the right-of-way. The unsuspecting buyer purchased the farm, not thinking to ask if someone had a right-of-way. One day when the new owner was relaxing in his living room, he spied a tractor coming up the laneway towards the house. He wondered who it might be, so he went out to investigate. Meanwhile, the tractor and driver had passed by the house, through the back yard and into a tiny field. The new owner of the farm followed. When the new owner asked the man what he was about, driving up his laneway and passing by the house to the little field at the back, the man on the tractor answered: "This small field is mine and I have legal right-of-way up the lane in order to reach this piece of property."

A right-of-way reduces the value of property significantly. The farmer who sold the property may have argued that he did not speak falsely about the situation. He simply did not tell the whole truth. Truth is that which corresponds to reality. The reality in this case was that a legal right-of-way existed, and the selling farmer withheld the information in favor of a better price for the farm. Sometimes the *whole* truth is hard to tell. Without it, people are blindsided as a result. The truth sets people free to live authentic lives. "Authenticity is the heart of the matter."[11]

No wonder the theme of truth in the Fourth Gospel is repeated numerous times. The alternative to truth is either outright falsehood, or a partial telling of the truth. The latter is much more subtle. Court judges and juries expect to hear the whole truth, and nothing but the truth. A missing piece of vital information is detrimental to the successful outcome of a case related to a defendant. Of course, there are pragmatic people who hold to the notion that where falsehood works to personal or institutional advantage, then use it instead of truth. There are myriad stories of people in highly respectable positions who treat truth and falsehood pragmatically: use whichever works to advantage. But that kind of pragmatism becomes a fool's paradise.

An acute problem arises when truth is fudged or ignored by religious leaders. When a pastor or priest instructs a congregation to live consistent lives in relation to Jesus, that pastor or priest is thereby expected to exhibit truth in everyday life outside the church or seminary classroom. More than a few church leaders have brought shame upon themselves, upon the institution they represent, and worst of all upon Jesus who is the way, the truth, and the life. The Jesus we encounter in the Fourth Gospel stands for truth, lives in truth, speaks truth. And what he speaks corresponds to his way of life-and-death. Those who claim to follow the path that Jesus walked, who preach to others about him and the path he followed, are thereby required by virtue of truth to operate by the high standard Jesus followed, even onto death. To argue, as some do, that it is impossible for human beings to follow truth as Jesus taught it, are apt to justify falsehood as an acceptable alternative for "imperfect" humankind. I find that line of argument unsustainable. Truth must operate within the human mind, and thereby within human society. Reality is at stake, without which human society cannot function.

Reality extends well beyond our personal lives, our particular country, and our beloved planet Earth. Every day I am thankful for scientists and scholars who have committed themselves to truth in various spheres of existence. The advances in medicine in my lifetime, for example, have been immense. People are living longer now than in any other era of human

---

11. Meyer, *Critical Realism*, 45.

history. Scientific achievements have become the flagship of our modern and postmodern age. But we still have some distance to go yet.

Our beloved planet Earth is suffering increasingly from global warming, according to our scientific colleagues. The millions of cars, tractors, trucks, trains, and airplanes that pollute Earth's atmosphere in our time are mindboggling. Some attempts are being made to reduce the use of fossil fuels for vehicles. Electric vehicles are beginning to appear, but all too slowly. If such an option is truly viable why does it take so long to adopt it? The truth about global warming needs to be taken more seriously by individuals and governments, and alternates found sooner rather than later. Planet Earth and its inhabitants—humans, animals, and plants—deserve to be set free from the pollutants in the atmosphere, and the warming that melts Earth's ice fields.

Beyond our planet Earth are myriad more planets and galaxies. The whole truth about all of them is beyond our capacity to comprehend fully. Physicists, astronomers, and geologists have discovered much about our place in solar system. No longer do we think of the Sun moving around the earth every twenty-four hours. No longer do we think of the Earth as flat. We trust the physicists and explorers to seek and find the truth on our behalf, because the truth about these and so many other aspects of reality sets us free. Big subjects like these require more than a paragraph or two. I site them here as elements of truth with which we should become familiar. To imagine a false universe is to be satisfied with a fool's paradise.

In short, the truth (*alêtheia*) about which Jesus spoke in the Fourth Gospel is about coming to terms with reality, not fiction and not falsehood. To treat truth and falsehood as equal alternatives, i.e., whichever works to personal advantage, leads to breakdown in communication, causing grief and pain. Seeking and finding truth, by contrast, sets the human spirit free to live authentically. It is sometimes said, "truth hurts." That may be so for a while, but truth is the balm that sets the human spirit free to bathe in the life-giving spirit of Jesus Messiah, according to the tone and texture of the Fourth Gospel.

A final word about *truth* in relation to *faith* in the Fourth Gospel will bring this chapter to a close. Truth and faith are not exactly incompatible. But the difference between the two needs to be recognized. As noted already, truth corresponds to reality. By "reality" I mean that which is *perceived* by the senses and *understood* to have an observable state of being across cultures. Faith, on the other hand, sees with the inner eye beyond that which the human senses perceive and understand. An individual's faith is usually supported by a community mind, together with texts and traditions from time past. As such, faith *imagines* beyond that which is observed by the human senses and corresponding insight. And for ardent believers such faith becomes as real as the air they breathe, the food they eat, and the house in which they live. Nevertheless, the difference needs to be recognized between the senses that perceive the physical world, and the eye of faith that "sees" an otherwise unseen world. What one culture group of people believes about that unseen world differs from what another culture group believes. So be it. The difference between the cultural groups is not a matter of truth versus falsehood. It is a difference of culture and belief. No one religious vision is absolute—one absolutely true and the other absolutely not.

Francis Bacon's judgment of Pilate's question is on target: he asked aright, but did not stay for an answer. Regrettably, others have since followed Pilate's example. To discover the answer we need to join heart and hand out of respect for each other, and together with one accord celebrate truth that sets the human spirit free. Jesus in the Fourth Gospel demonstrated the essential character of truth in his way of life and thought, in his loving concern for people in need, and in his profound relationship to a sovereign God.

13

Playing Politics: The Case Against Jesus

THE TIME OF JESUS "was the best of times, it was the worst of times," to quote Charles Dickens. It was a time when two highly charged political cities were in tension with each other, the Jewish city of Jerusalem and the imperial city of Rome. The power politics of Rome dominated the Mediterranean basin and beyond, while Jerusalem laid claim to a long religious-political history. Jewish adulation for kings David and Solomon of past history was deeply ingrained in the Jewish psyche of the time, and came into play in bringing a case against Jesus. Both kings of Israel ruled the kingdom centered in Jerusalem in turn, but at the time of Jesus there was no king and no nation of Israel.

Jerusalem had fallen under Roman occupation and rule. Pilate was Rome's representative in Judea. Then came Jesus into the middle of the political fray announcing a new kind of kingdom. His was not militaristic, not constituted by human ingenuity, not seeking to overcome an enemy nation, and not at all like Caesar's kingdom. The kingdom that Jesus announced and enacted in his ministry was none other than the kingdom of God, and Jesus himself its vice-regent. "Kingdom" (*basileia*) was a highly charged political term in any part of the Roman Empire, and nowhere more so than in Palestinian Jerusalem.

A Complicated Love Story

FROM INNOCENT LIFE TO IGNOMINIOUS DEATH

This section focuses on a series of movements found in chapters 18 and 19 of the Fourth Gospel, which led ultimately to the death of Jesus by crucifixion. It is instructive to follow the steps highlighted below insofar as they help identify the sensitive balance that existed between the two political cities of Jerusalem and Rome. Jesus, having called twelve male followers representative of Israel restored, found himself caught in the political crosshairs operating among the representatives of the two cities, Rome and Jerusalem.

ARREST IN AN OLIVE GARDEN

The Mount of Olives lies east of the Kidron Valley, over against the city of Jerusalem. There was an olive garden at the bottom of the mountain where Jesus was wont to go for quiet reflection and prayer. The Fourth Evangelist makes no mention of Jesus praying in the garden, asking God to take the cup of suffering away from him (cf. Mark 14:36; Matt 26:39; Luke 22:42). On the contrary, the Fourth Evangelist records the opposite emotion and purpose of Jesus: "Now my soul is troubled. And what should I say—'Father, save me from this hour'? No, it is for this reason that I have come to this hour" (12:27). This spiritual and psychological posture of Jesus echoes the synoptic prayer of Jesus to Father God to remove the cup of suffering from him, but only so as to cancel out such a plea from the mind and lips of Jesus.

We come now to the part Judas played in the arrest of Jesus in the garden. Judas is depicted as a person of the darkness, as compared to "the light of the world" projected in the life and ministry of Jesus (8:12; 9:5). At the last meal with his disciples Jesus identified Judas as the disciple who would betray him. It is then said that Judas went out from the group after the supper was finished. "And it was night" (13:30). This is in sharp contrast to the very positive symbol of light in the Fourth Gospel. So we glean from this and other negative depictions of Judas that he was characteristically a dark and forceful figure among the disciples. Yet Jesus had called him to make up the symbolic (if not political) group of twelve. Jesus also entrusted Judas with the funds needed for food and shelter along the way.

Judas knew where to find Jesus. He had been to the olive garden with Jesus on other occasions. So he got in touch with some Roman soldiers together with police backed by the Jewish Sanhedrin, and led the joint contingent to the garden. The joint cohort "came there with lanterns and torches and weapons" (18:3). Whatever motivated Judas to betray Jesus into the hands of the two authorities is puzzling and perplexing. He doubtless heard Jesus talk about a coming kingdom of peace. And Judas, being a disciple of Jesus, may have tried to force his hand to hasten the inauguration of that new kingdom sooner rather than later. That Judas betrayed Jesus into the hands of the soldiers and police out of a wicked heart and selfish motive is debatable. True enough, Matthew records him taking thirty pieces of silver as payment for his betrayal of Jesus (Matt 30:15). But when the betrayal failed to persuade Jesus to enact the new kingdom, Judas threw the silver coins back at the chief priests and elders. His plan to force Jesus's hand had failed. So he promptly went out and hanged himself, presumably out of profound grief for his misguided plan to force Jesus's hand (Matt 27:5). I suggest that Judas was exceedingly presumptuous and power-hungry. In that sense he misconstrued the selfless, peace-loving character of Jesus and the kingdom of God that he preached.

PROFOUND SIGNIFICANCE OF "I AM"

As noted in earlier chapters, "I am" in the voice of Jesus signals something supernatural, beyond time and place; beyond change and chance. And nowhere in the Fourth Gospel is that image more striking than in the scene of the arrest of Jesus in the olive garden. Soldiers and police entered into the space that Jesus occupied. They came "with lanterns and torches and weapons" to arrest Jesus (18:3). He asked them who they were trying to arrest. They said "Jesus of Nazareth." Jesus went along with that identity, even though Nazareth is a poor peasant village in Galilee. Recall Nathaniel's comment at 1:14 about the identity of Jesus of Nazareth: "Can anything good come out of Nazareth?" Jesus had grown up in that insignificant village as a devout Jew. But it was the particular way he identified himself that seemingly struck the soldiers, making them fall to the ground.

Jesus had used a heavily freighted phrase consisting of two little Greek words; three in the English NRSV: "I am he" (*ego eimi*, 18:6). From our perspective it seems like a simple way to respond to the soldiers and police. But as we know from reading the previous chapters of the Fourth Gospel, the two-word phrase carries great weight. The two Greek words are existential in character. *Ego eimi* translates as "I am." Jesus is the existent one; the one who is! In other words, the inner character of Jesus is timeless, whether he remains alive in the flesh or is physically killed. Timeless one.

When the soldiers heard the "I am" they fell to the ground. What a strange reaction to such a simple phrase. And the narrator does not help us understand the sense of such reaction from the soldiers. Why would Roman soldiers understand the significance of "I am"? The astute reader or listener will get it. That is especially so if they have read the text of Exodus 3:14: "God said to Moses, 'I AM WHO I AM.' He said further, 'Thus you shall say to the Israelites, "I AM has sent me to you."'" The God of Israel is the Existent One who transcends history with its ebb and flow, its pain and pleasure, its change and decay . . . And the character of Jesus aligns with the character of that God as son to father. Hence the soldiers "stepped back and fell to the ground" when they heard the eternal "I am" in the voice of Jesus of Nazareth (18:6). That is how the Fourth Evangelist perceives Jesus: God's eternal vice-regent existing within the universal world.

SIMON PETER'S PERSONAL MILITARISM

In his characteristic way in this Fourth Gospel, Jesus singularly bears the burden and the brunt of arrest by Roman soldiers. His concern was for the others who followed him in his mission. "Let these men go," he says to the soldiers (18:8). In this instruction to the soldiers we witness the self-giving character of Jesus: he is more concerned for the well-being of his disciples than for his own. In hindsight, though, we realize the far-reaching significance of this word of Jesus on behalf of his followers. After Jesus's death his disciples carried the mission of Jesus forward well beyond what Jesus started. The Jewish community of Jesus Messiah multiplied increasingly in Jerusalem and beyond in the centuries that followed, to ultimately become the world religion it is today, made up mostly of non-Jewish members.

Still within the garden setting where the arrest of Jesus took place, we are confronted with an unlikely incident of violence coming from a principal disciple of Jesus, Simon Peter. The incident is narrated in few words, leaving us with questions not easily answered from the slight description within the scene. "Simon Peter, who had a sword, drew it, struck the high priest's slave, and cut off his right ear."(18:10). Here is a sample of the kinds of questions this brief episode raises. Why was Peter carrying a sword? Was he aiming at the slave's right ear or his carotid artery? If Jesus taught his disciples the good news of love and peace, what are we to make of Simon Peter's attack on a slave-soldier using a deadly weapon? Perhaps Simon Peter carried the sword to ward off wild animals while the disciples journeyed here and there in Palestine. We really don't know the answer.

This much we do know. Jesus did not approve of Peter's militaristic action on this occasion of arrest. "Put your sword back into its sheath," said Jesus. "Am I not to drink the cup that the Father has given me?" (18:11). (According to Luke 22:53 Jesus healed the slave's ear.) The response from Jesus raises yet another puzzling question, or two. What is the meaning of the metaphor of drinking "the cup that the Father has given me"? In the setting of arrest and trial and impending execution, the cup most likely signals the suffering and/or death of Jesus. If this is so, as seems likely, why would it be necessary for the gracious God and Father of the Lord Jesus Christ to inflict such suffering and death on his beloved Son? This is yet another sticky theological question for which there is no truly satisfactory answer. I have heard it said, "God killed his son, Jesus, to save the sinful people of the world." The doctrine is sometimes called substitutionary atonement: the sacrifice of the innocent one to save the many who are guilty. But is not the killing of one innocent person a sinful act? One can understand how this doctrine would become theologically problematic.

INTERROGATED BY TWO HIGH PRIESTS

There were two high priests working in tandem at the time, so it seems. Annas, father-in-law to Caiaphas, first questioned Jesus about his disciples and his teaching (18:19). The motive for such questioning, presumably, was to determine if Jesus was teaching radical and dangerous lessons to the Jewish people living under Roman domination in Palestine. It was not merely a matter of preserving right Jewish doctrine and tradition. It was as much a political matter of ensuring that Jesus and his followers were not teaching sedition against Rome. Again, the balance of power was always tenuous, and carefully monitored. Jesus provided guarded answers to Annas's questions about his teaching: "I have spoken openly to the world; I have always taught in synagogues and in the temple, where all the Jews come together. I have said nothing in secret. Why do you ask me? Ask those who heard what I said to them; they know what I said" (18:20–21). In other words, Jesus was not agitating people to rise up in protest against Jewish or Roman power in Palestine. So he defends himself before Annas of the Sanhedrin against such political jockeying.

Annas then transferred Jesus bound to Caiaphas, the high priest that year (18:13). One would expect Caiaphas to question Jesus diligently about political aspects in his preaching and teaching. And one would think the narrator of the Fourth Gospel would let the reader in on his questions to Jesus as well Jesus's answers. But there is no such record of the interrogation in the Fourth Gospel. Caiaphas is best known for his one-line dictum, recorded in two places in the Fourth Gospel. Speaking to members of the Sanhedrin he states, "You do not understand that it is better for you to have one man die for the people than to have the whole nation destroyed" (11:50; 18:14). In the earlier setting of 11:50 we meet Caiaphas and members of the Sanhedrin grappling with a real concern of the Jewish leaders about the radical ministry of Jesus in Palestine: how to avoid an uprising against Rome. It seems that's how it was in the minds of the Jewish leaders. We have a sampling of their real concern about Jesus at 11:47–48. "What are we to do?" the members of the Jewish council asked. "This man is performing many signs. If we let him go on like this, everyone will believe in him, and the Romans will come and destroy both our holy place and our nation." There it is in bold relief. Members of the Jewish council are trying to preserve the security of the Jewish people in Palestine, and with them the sacred space for worship in the temple of Jerusalem. In short, they fear a deadly assault perpetrated by the Romans, which did happen eventually in 66 CE. So Caiaphas has the solution to the Palestinian Jewish quandary: "It is better for you to have one man die for the people than to have the whole nation destroyed." And as the Jewish trial continued, the Roman governor, Pilate, stood outside ready and waiting to carry out their dictum about the one for the many.

INTERROGATED BY THE ROMAN, PILATE

"Then [the Jewish police] took Jesus from Caiaphas to Pilate's headquarters. It was early in the morning. They themselves did not enter the headquarters [of Pilate], so as to avoid ritual defilement and to be able to eat the Passover" (18:28). Pilate purportedly asked the Jewish council members to judge Jesus themselves according to their own law, but the Jewish judges refused. They maintained that they were not permitted to put anyone to death. Presumably they meant death by crucifixion. Crucifixion was practiced by the Persians, and then also by the Romans. It was used not only as a form of severe punishment, but also as a deterrent against crimes, especially those against the empire. Both cross and victim were placed in plain sight for passersby to witness, and thereby steer clear of such ignominious death. The crucified victims did not die from loss of blood, but from asphyxiation, which happened when they could no longer hold themselves up by their feet and legs.

When Pilate had Jesus in the headquarters, he interrogated him about his mission and his identity. However many questions Pilate may have asked Jesus, one in particular was crucial. Pilate doubtless heard rumblings about Jesus's teaching concerning the kingdom of God. Hence his loaded question to Jesus: "Are you the King of the Jews?" (18:33). From Pilate's perspective that question is not a religious one, nor a hypothetical one. It is critically political. Jesus replied in a guarded way, as he had done when the high priest questioned him. This time he stands before powerful Pilate who values his appointment as Roman prefect of Judea. Jesus answered broadly in the affirmative: "My kingdom is not from this world. If my kingdom were from this world, my followers would be fighting to keep me from being handed over to the Jews. But as it is, my kingdom is not from here" (18:36). In other words, the kind of kingdom Jesus represents is a peaceable kingdom. Yet Pilate is not quite satisfied with that soft manner of explanation. So he asks again more broadly: "So you are a king?" (18:37).

Jesus does not deny it. But he qualifies his response to Pilate's unvarnished question. "You say that I am a king. For this I was born, and for this I came into the world, to testify to the truth. Everyone who belongs to the truth listens to my voice" (18:37). And as we found in the previous chapter, Pilate asked an important question about the definition of truth but did not stay for the answer.

Pilate then turned his attention to the Jewish judges from the Sanhedrin. His questions were more of a taunt than real inquiry. "Do you want me to release for you the King of the Jews?" (18:39). I suggest that Pilate was testing the members of the Sanhedrin as to their allegiance to Caesar. Had they said "Yes" in response to Pilate he would then know their inclination towards self-rule led by one of their own people. But apparently, the leading Jews were able to read Pilate's motive for asking his loaded question. So they answered in a way that saved their people of Palestine and their temple of Jerusalem. They asked to have a renegade bandit, Barabbas, released to them instead of Jesus. Barabbas posed no major political threat.

Then Pilate had Jesus flogged. Meanwhile, Pilate's Roman soldiers, knowing his propensity for inflicting pain on his victims, were weaving a bunch of thorns into a mock crown. They put the thorny crown on Jesus's head. They struck him on the face. They taunted him with mocking jibes: "Hail, King of the Jews!" (19:3). They also put a purple robe on him, another mocking symbol. Then after all of this mocking and taunting, Pilate came out to the Jewish leaders with Jesus nearby, and said, "Here is the man!" (19:5): humiliated, disgraced, powerless Jesus of Nazareth. Imagine how this bleeding, broken king appeared to the Jewish priests and people. The Jewish hierarchy reminded Pilate "If you release this man, you are no friend of the emperor. Everyone who claims to be a king sets himself against the emperor" (19:12). As if Pilate did not know that already, he said yet again, "Here is your king" (14:12). A beaten, beleaguered, bleeding figure of a man is the only king you have, implied Pilate. So the Jewish leaders cried out to Pilate to crucify him. "Shall I crucify your king?" asked mocking Pilate. And on that deadly note, he wrung from their lips precisely what he wanted to hear from them: "We have no king but the emperor" (19:15). At that critical juncture in the proceedings, Pilate handed Jesus over to be crucified. Ironically, that was the day of Preparation for Passover, a high and holy holiday in Judaism, then as now. Passover celebrates the liberation of the ancient Hebrews from bondage in Egypt.

JESUS CARRIED HIS CROSS

According to the three Synoptic Gospels, Jesus was not obliged to carry his cross to the place of execution. The soldiers who beat him, and otherwise abused him, compelled a man from the country, Simon from Cyrene, to carry the cross of Jesus to the designated spot. Some people guess that Jesus was so worn out from the abuse he suffered that he was unable to carry his cross (Mark 15:21; Matt. 27:32; Luke 23:6).

The Fourth Evangelist, however, appears to take issue with that understanding of the event presented in the other three Gospels. I think it would serve well to lay out that text about Jesus carrying the cross himself. The sentence structure implies that the Fourth Evangelist knew the Synoptic Gospels, and modified their scenario thus: "So they took Jesus; and carrying the cross by himself, he went out to what is called The Place of the Skull, which in Hebrew is called Golgotha" (19:16–17). The implied sense is that Jesus bore in his own body the full weight of suffering for the sake of others. This nuance about carrying his own cross has a similar ring to the other situation—cited previously—about Jesus's prayer in the olive garden of Gethsemane concerning the cup of suffering. In the Fourth Gospel, he refuses to pray for the cup of suffering to be averted. Instead, he prays the opposite in his hour of trouble: "And what should I say—'Father, save me from this hour'? No, it is for this reason that I have come to this hour" (12:27; cf. Matt. 26:39; Mark 14:36; Luke 22:42).

PILATE WROTE A PROVOCATIVE INSCRIPTION FOR THE TOP

We come now to Pilate's highly provocative inscription placed over the head of Jesus on the cross: "Jesus of Nazareth, the King of the Jews" (19:19). The text was written in Hebrew, in Latin, and in Greek, and thus applicable to every passerby. Unlike the Synoptic Gospels, the Fourth Gospel clearly places motivation for the inscription unequivocally in Pilate's mind and heart. We need to understand clearly the function of a public crucifixion at a prominent place. It was meant as punishment on the victim to be sure, but it also served as a deterrent against such criminal intent among the people. At least that was the hope in the minds of politicians and court judges of the time. It was certainly the intent of Pilate in the crucifixion of Jesus. Implicitly the inscription over the head of Jesus aimed at having the passersby say to themselves, "I want to avoid such painful crucifixion, no matter what!"

But this particular inscription on top of the cross of Jesus was an extraordinary one. It was not every day that someone in Judea, or elsewhere in Roman-occupied Palestine, would claim to be the Anointed (Messiah) King in keeping with the will of Creator God. Such a king outranks not only Governor Pilate in Palestine, but also his Imperial Highness, Tiberius of Rome. In writing the inscription as he does, according to the Fourth Gospel, Pilate ridicules the absurdity of Jesus's claim to be king of the Jews. He is "Jesus of Nazareth," an insignificant village in Galilee. Of the many villages of Palestine recorded in the writings of Josephus, Nazareth is not among them. Yet that little village was the one in which Jesus had lived with his family for about twenty-five years. People were often identified according to their place of regular abode. The same holds to some extent in the present time. The queen of the United Kingdom lives in Buckingham Palace in the major city of London, England. Jesus lived in little insignificant Nazareth in the region of Galilee. Pilate was not merely identifying Jesus's place of origin as a piece of objective knowledge. He was defining the status and worth of the victim on the cross. He depicted Jesus of Nazareth as a person of low birth and upbringing, undeserving of the status of kingship. His placard derided Jesus and effectively warned the observers not to follow suit.

The chief priests of the Jewish elite approached Pilate with a possible revision of his inscription. They said to Pilate, "Do not write, 'The King of the Jews,' but, 'This man said, I am King of the Jews'" (19:21). Pilate didn't budge from his initial text of the inscription. What he infamously said in reply to the Jewish revisionists was unequivocal. "What I have written I have written" (19:22). In other words, this crucified, bleeding, suffering king is the only kind of king that the Jewish people of Israel will ever have while I am governor of Judea.

While Jesus poured out his earthly life on the cross for the sake of others, all but one of his disciples fled the scene, according to the Fourth Evangelist. Apparently, the disciples were not prepared to identify with the crucified suffering-servant Messiah-King on public display. Their confidence grew eventually when the ignominy of their crucified Savior had vanished from public display. So they were able to talk to people everywhere about the past suffering and death of their Messiah, Jesus, without fear of recrimination.

14

Temporary Tomb

WE HAVE NO CLUE from the Fourth Gospel who owned the tomb in which the pierced body of Jesus was laid. It was important to the Jewish leaders to have the dead body removed from the cross and entombed before the day of Preparation. That special day happened once a year as forerunner to one of the most significant Jewish holidays of the year: *Passover*. Remembering the event of the first Passover in Egypt from so long ago became a hallmark of Jewish identity, and remains so to this day. It signaled freedom from bondage and hard labor. On this particular occasion of Passover it seems that members of Jesus's family were not on hand to remove the body of Jesus from the cross and transport it to the "family cave." It was customary and important for the head of a Jewish family at the time to lay claim to a burial place, often a cave, for members of the family. The supporting text that undergirds this brief introduction to the situation in the Fourth Gospel should be in plain view for reference as follows:

> Since it was the day of Preparation [for Passover], the Jews did not want the bodies left on the cross during the sabbath, especially because that sabbath was a day of great solemnity . . .
>
> After these things, Joseph of Arimathea, who was a disciple of Jesus, though a secret one because of his fear of the Jews, asked Pilate to let him take away the body of Jesus. Pilate gave him permission; so he came and removed his body. Nicodemus, who had at first come to Jesus by night, also came, bringing a mixture of myrrh and aloes, weighing about a hundred pounds. They [Joseph and Nicodemus] took the body of Jesus and wrapped it with the

spices in linen cloths, according to the burial custom of the Jews. Now there was a garden in the place where he was crucified, and in the garden there was a new tomb in which no one had ever been laid. And so, because it was the Jewish day of Preparation, and the tomb was nearby, they laid Jesus there. (19:31–42)

COMPARATIVE ACCOUNTS RELATED TO JOSEPH OF ARIMATHEA

Let's be clear about the historical place of the Fourth Gospel in relation to the other three Gospels. The three are generally referred to as "Synoptic" (lit. "seeing with one eye") insofar as the three have significant texts in common. This togetherness is not always word-for-word copying. One of the three was first, and the other two used the earliest one as a base on which to build a larger body of literature about the good news of Jesus. When the copyist disagreed with the precise wording of the source document, that writer would change the wording accordingly. But which of the three Gospels was first? The general consensus today is that Mark was the earliest Gospel, and that the authors of Matthew and Luke gathered material from Mark as a base for their expanded Gospels respectively.

My reason for drafting this brief note about the interrelatedness of the three Synoptic Gospels at this juncture is because the figure of Joseph of Arimathea in relation to the body of Jesus appears in all four Gospels, but not identically so. It is generally held that the Fourth Gospel is chronologically fourth in relation to the other three. In other words, the author of the Fourth Gospel probably had access to all three, and used them minimally and strategically along with other information to create a distinct document about the ministry of Jesus, including his death, burial, and resurrection. Clearly, the object of this present book is to peer inside the implied mind of the Fourth Evangelist as far as possible. But the way the subject matter in chapter 19 unfolds calls for comparison with the other three partners. If there is tension between them, so be it. Let it stand within the frame of reference implied in the respective Gospel. Attempts at harmonizing the Gospels have not honored the respective writers, but have, instead, satisfied the interpreter whose view of Scripture requires complete coherence in all its parts. Diligent truth-seekers, less constrained by traditional doctrine, allow for difference among the three.

The aim is to garner insight into each author's possible motive behind the difference, and interpret accordingly.

Compare the similarity and difference between the four aligned texts below on the subject of Joseph of Arimathea and the empty tomb in the garden.

Mark 15:45–46	Matt 27:57	Luke 23:50	FG 19:40–42
When [Pilate] learned from the centurion that [Jesus] was dead, he granted the body to Joseph of Arimathea. Then Joseph bought a linen cloth, and taking down the body, wrapped it in the linen cloth, and laid it in a tomb that had been hewn out of the rock. He then rolled a stone against the door of the tomb.	[Joseph of Arimathea] went to Pilate and asked for the body of Jesus; then Pilate ordered it to be given to him. So Joseph took the body and wrapped it in a clean linen cloth and laid it in his own new tomb, which he had hewn in the rock. He then rolled a great stone to the door of the tomb and went away.	[Joseph of Arimathea] was waiting expectantly for the kingdom of God. This man went to Pilate and asked for the body of Jesus. Then he took it down, wrapped it in a linen cloth, and laid it in a rock-hewn tomb where no one had ever been laid.	[Joseph of Arimathea and Nicodemus] took the body of Jesus and wrapped it with the spices in linen cloths . . . Now there was a garden in the place where he was crucified, and in the garden there was a new tomb in which no one had ever been laid. And so, because it was the Jewish day of Preparation, and the tomb was nearby, they laid Jesus there.

Observe both the similarity and difference between the four excerpts above taken from the four Gospels.

Mark tells us that the tomb was hewn out of rock, and that Joseph rolled a stone against the door. There is no mention of either of these in the Fourth Gospel. Mark does not draw attention to the close proximity of the tomb to the place of crucifixion. The Fourth Gospel does not speak of the tomb being hewn out of rock, nor the rolling of a stone in front of the opening.

Matthew alone highlights the idea that Joseph laid the body of Jesus "in his own new tomb." Presumably, Matthew had some problem with Mark's Joseph seizing a convenient tomb, not his own, for the body of Jesus. Otherwise Matthew follows Mark's narrative. The Fourth Gospel is closer to Mark's description than to Matthew's.

Luke, while following Mark closely, is inclined to highlight Joseph of Arimathea as a genuine follower of Jesus in that he was "waiting expectantly for the kingdom of God," a major theme of Jesus's ministry, present already in Mark 15:43. The Fourth Gospel does not connect Joseph directly with this kingdom theme.

The Fourth Evangelist treats the action of Joseph of Arimathea, accompanied by Nicodemus, in a more pragmatic way. (The other three Evangelists do not mention Nicodemus anywhere in their Gospels). The body of Jesus had to be taken down from the cross in preparation for the high holiday fast approaching. Joseph was eager to show respect to Jesus, having become a disciple of his teaching. So Joseph, being "a respected member of the council" (Mark 15:43), dared to ask Pilate for the body of Jesus.

No one else was available at the time to take the body of Jesus down and give it a proper burial in a family tomb. Or if they were available they may have feared a negative consequence of asking Pilate for the body. Some credit goes to Joseph of Arimathea for his respect for the crucified body of Jesus. In that light, and with the High Holiday fast approaching, placing the body of Jesus in the nearby tomb in the garden comes across in the Fourth Gospel as an emergency measure. As noted already, none of Jesus's family came at the beginning of the High Holiday to take the body of Jesus to its proper resting place in the family tomb. The tomb in the nearby garden merely served as a temporary measure until the family members were able to give Jesus a proper burial in the family tomb secured for such a time and circumstance as this. That is how it appears to me. The Fourth Evangelist noticeably does not highlight a circular stone being rolled in front of the tomb, although it doubtless was, as implied in the sketch about Mary Magdalene coming to the tomb and finding the stone rolled away from the front of the tomb (20:1).

CONCERNING THE BODY OF JESUS

The impression I get from reading this burial text in the Fourth Gospel is that the nearby garden tomb was merely a convenient stopgap measure executed with speed by Joseph of Arimathea in preparation for the special Sabbath festival fast approaching. The crucified body of the Jewish Jesus in plain view during the festival of Passover would evoke certain shame directed at those who voted for such a cruel execution of a recognized Jewish teacher. A pressing question comes to mind about the burial of

Jesus, and the note that the temporary tomb was empty by the time Mary Magdalene arrived on Sunday morning. A down-to-earth response to that observation might well be that those close to Jesus, particularly some family members, came to the garden under cover of darkness early Sunday morning to take the body of Jesus from the temporary tomb ahead of Mary's arrival at the scene.

While this scenario may not satisfy all readers, I prefer it to the suggestion made by Malcolm Muggeridge in his book, *Jesus Rediscovered*. He believed some robbers had heard about the crucifixion of a king, which suggested to them that there would be jewels and gold on the body. The robbers then came to the tomb under cover of darkness and decamped with the body to a desert place. When they examined the body they found nothing of consequence, so they left the body and bones of Jesus in the desert "to whiten in the sun, those precious, precious bones." I disagree with this fanciful conjecture. It implicitly disparages the family of Jesus beyond measure. We have seen in a previous chapter that brother James continued the ministry of Jesus in Jerusalem with remarkable success for as long as possible. We have found also in Acts chapter 1 that the mother and brothers of Jesus were in an upstairs room awaiting the descent of the Spirit upon them, post-resurrection. To ignore the love of the family of Jesus toward their beloved brother and son is to disparage them without cause.

One thing is clear from the relevant texts: no one on record witnessed the resurrection of Jesus as an observable event. Christians who highlight "the empty tomb" as evidence for the resurrection of the *physical* body of Jesus to the same state as before the crucifixion should rethink that conviction. Here's why. The physical body of the historical Jesus was mortal, subject to all the sensory experiences to which human flesh is heir, including aging and death. If "resurrection" means a return to the same kind of body as before crucifixion, then nothing was gained by Jesus's death-and-resurrection. Such a resurrected one would be as time-bound and humanly restricted as before. In that case, there would be no difference between the raising of Lazarus and the resurrection of Jesus. But there was a marked difference, as we shall discover further in the next chapter. The new form of Jesus resurrected transcended a mortal body of flesh and blood and bone, which is invariably subject to suffering and death. The resurrected Jesus "appeared" to believers unawares, and disappeared in the same fashion. His former body of restricted flesh and bone and blood had given way to an unrestricted body suited to eternal life. To suggest otherwise would leave members of the human family, whom God loves, in the same state of physical mortality, without hope of eternal life.

This conversation requires another chapter devoted to the important subject of the saving grace of Jesus resurrected on behalf of human family. And so it shall be.

15

The Reality of Jesus Resurrected

THE MORE ONE PROBES the complex subject of resurrection, that of Jesus in particular, the more one confronts inexplicable mystery. Some well-meaning "believers," whether Jewish, Christian, Muslim, or otherwise, become disturbed by the idea that mystery belongs to faith. But the plain truth is that the words faith, belief, and trust imply an undiscovered realm of reality beyond empirical observation, beyond reason, beyond science: a realm that presents itself to our minds in part. None of us knows all there is to know about the eternal God, any more than we know all there is to know about outer space. According to Elizabeth Howell, "The universe is expanding faster than the speed of light," which implies we cannot ever know all there is to know about the myriad galaxies, much less all there is to know about Creator God. But we know enough about God to exercise faith. We also know that the vast realm of the eternal in which God resides is a known unknown. Now I am beginning to sound a bit like the apostle Paul.

Paul probed the subject of resurrection with the rest of us mortals, and left us with his tentative conclusion on the matter, one that we would do well to emulate: "For we know only in part, and we prophesy only in part; but when the complete comes, the partial will come to an end. When I was a child, I spoke like a child, I thought like a child, I reasoned like a child; when I became an adult, I put an end to childish ways. For now we see in a mirror, dimly, but then we will see face to face. Now I know only in part; then I will know fully, even as I have been fully known" (1 Cor 13:9–13).

I have chosen to peruse the topic of this chapter along four lines of thought with a view to capturing the uniqueness and significance of Jesus's resurrection and "appearances."

JESUS RESURRECTED COMPARED TO LAZARUS RESTORED

As we discovered in chapter 8, the raising of Lazarus was an extraordinary miracle performed by Jesus. Apart from the action-and-word of Jesus there was not the slightest hope for the return of Lazarus to his daily life in Bethany in the home of his two sisters. That is the clear impression arising out of the narrative. Sister Martha even informs Jesus about the length of time Lazarus had been entombed before Jesus arrived on the scene. In short, the possibility of bringing Lazarus back to this family and home was hopeless by common consensus. By contrast, in the matter of Jesus's resurrection from the dead there is no record of a miracle being performed by someone else, no powerful word uttered by anyone to make the miracle happen, and not a hint about who moved the stone. All of that distinguishes the raising of Lazarus from the resurrection of Jesus. Implicitly for Jesus there was power beyond human word and deed, power that generated a new kind of life for him, no longer subject to pain of crucifixion resulting in death. Moreover, the miraculous raising of Lazarus from the dead, extraordinary as it was, does not measure up to the unaided resurrection of Jesus.

It bears repeating that the miracle of the raising of Lazarus had many witnesses to the event. Martha was there, of course, and also Mary. But there was also a number of Jews present at the scene. They had come to mourn with the sisters, and now they were on hand to witness Jesus as lifegiver for the restoration of Lazarus to his familiar place at Bethany. Before the miracle happened, however, the Jews observed how much Jesus loved his good friend. Concerning the resurrection of Jesus, by comparison, there was not a single witness on hand to testify to what really happened, and none to experience the transformation of the body of Jesus from mortal flesh and blood to an immortal state of grace and power. The account of Lazarus restored to life should be viewed as a "sign," a very significant sign indeed in the Book of Signs. On the other hand, the resurrection of Jesus from among the dead, testifies to a kind of life belonging to eternal reality for which suffering humanity longs.

The Reality of Jesus Resurrected

UNDERSTANDING "APPEARANCE"

Lazarus did not miraculously "appear" to people following his death and burial. When Jesus arrived at Bethany, Lazarus was still in the tomb. He had been there four days. Jesus asked the people nearby to remove the stone from the entrance to the tomb. When they had moved the stone, Jesus cried out, "Lazarus come forth." And he did come forth at the word of Jesus. He had trouble walking, bound as he was with the strips of cloth wrapped around him. So Jesus asked those nearby to "Unbind him, and let him go." And some friends then untied the strips of cloth and set him free. And there he was before the eyes of those gathered near the cave, those who had known him before his death. They all recognized his person right away, and knew his identity immediately. His natural life had been restored. Then it was time for dinner. Martha had prepared something for the group. They all reclined around the table to rejoice with Mary, Martha, and Lazarus. He reclined at the table with the rest of the folks in the house, and he ate the food that Martha had prepared. Jesus was there too, eating dinner with his friends, which now included his friend Lazarus, whom Jesus loved.

Now I ask: Was this a resurrection on par with that of Jesus that followed a week later? Not so. It could be called a miracle, yes, but not resurrection equal to that of Jesus. The raising of Lazarus was another "sign" merely, but not the reality of resurrected life on par with that of Jesus. Lazarus was still subject to death some time later. His restored life was still mortal. The resurrected Jesus was not. Lazarus did not simply and suddenly appear to people who knew him, and then disappear as suddenly and as mysteriously. The resurrected Jesus did so. He was no longer subject to physical pain and death. But how are we to understand the "appearances"?

APPEARANCE NARRATIVES IN ACTS AND THE FOURTH GOSPEL

All of the New Testament documents were written some years after the death of Jesus, some of them many years later. The Fourth Gospel, for example, was probably written at the turn of the first to the second century, some sixty or seventy years after the crucifixion of Jesus. Acts was likely written some years earlier, at about 85–90 CE. The letters of Paul are the earliest writings of the New Testament, about twenty to thirty years after the death of Jesus. I mention this temporal dimension of the resources we have, to highlight the point that the disciples' experience of Jesus resurrected was not set aside by them with the passing of time. Something extraordinary really happened to spur on the remaining disciples. It was memorable, and undeniable to people of faith in the saving grace of God in the person of Jesus Messiah.

Let me begin this little foray with the report in Acts 1:3: "After his suffering [Jesus] presented himself alive to [the disciples] by many convincing proofs, *appearing* to them during forty days and speaking about the kingdom of God." What the disciples experienced during those forty days, apparently, was the same Jesus with the same message, but coming to them in a new resurrected form. And the author of Acts, writing towards the end of the first century, does not fudge the reality of the disciples' experience during the forty days. Something really happened to spur the disciples forward in their mission, to bring the news to all Jerusalem and to the world. Jesus appeared to them, not as a ghost, not as premonition, nor as a dream in the night, but as a new spirit-empowered reality with heavenly meaning: Jesus as they had known him, and yet Jesus as they had not known him before.

We come now to appearances in the fourth Gospel. Jesus appeared first to a woman, Mary from Magdala in Galilee (20:13–18). This woman from Magdala was devoted to Jesus. She had traveled about 190 kilometers to Jerusalem for no other apparent reason than to be close to Jesus. She was a disciple who witnessed his crucifixion on Friday, and now early Sunday morning she has reached the tomb where his body was laid to rest on Friday evening. Then the unexpected happened. Jesus resurrected *appears* on the scene. But now Mary, who knew Jesus well, did not recognize him. Not at first. She thought he was the gardener. Why could she not recognize the one to whom she was so devoted for some time? I do not have an adequate answer. Apparently she needed a revelation. And she had a revelation when Jesus spoke her name. He was the same Jesus, yet not at all the same. She may have held onto Jesus earlier, but not this time. Jesus was in transition from earth and time and humanity to glorious eternity, where there is no more pain or death. Mary hurries to tell the brothers, probably the brothers of Jesus, or the disciples, or both. In any case, the word about the newness of life in Jesus resurrected needs to be broadcast among those who are able to see beyond the mundane. And a woman from Galilee was the first to see Jesus resurrected.

So Mary received a revelation of the resurrected Jesus early on Sunday morning. Then comes the evening of the same day. The disciples had gathered in a house somewhere in Jerusalem. The point is made that they locked the door after they had entered the house, because they were afraid of some Jewish leaders, probably members of the Sanhedrin who had sealed the death warrant of Jesus before Pontius Pilate on Friday. Within that secured house, Jesus suddenly appeared to them, and revealed to them that he was truly their Lord and Savior. A locked door no longer kept him on the outside. He simply appeared to them, and they recognized him as the one who had given his life as ransom for them, and for the many that would follow after them (Mark 10:45). From then on the faith-filled followers of Jesus would have his Holy Spirit to guide them into the way of truth and justice and peace. He gave them the enabling Spirit to carry forward the good news of grace and truth and hope into a benighted world.

One week later the same disciples were in the house. This time Thomas was with them. Thomas was known as the one who needed proof before he could bank his life on an endeavor, and I think I understand his position. There was Thomas in the room behind locked doors. Suddenly Jesus appears with a benediction for all of them: "Peace be with you." Then he asked Thomas to put his finger where the nails used to be, and his hand where the sword had pierced his side. Did doubting Thomas do such a thing? Hardly. He simply uttered profession of faith: "My Lord and my God."

PAUL'S VIEWS OF THE RESURRECTION AND APPEARANCE OF JESUS

The apostle Paul also confirms what we find in the Fourth Gospel about appearances of the resurrected Jesus. Paul himself was privileged to have such an appearance of the risen Jesus, an experience that changed the course of his life. Here is his testimony about the appearances: The risen Jesus "appeared to Peter, then to the twelve. Then he appeared to more than five hundred brothers and sisters at one time, most of whom are still alive, though some have died. Then he appeared to James, [the Lord's brother], then to all the apostles. Last of all, as to one untimely born, he appeared also to me" (1 Cor 15:5–8). The appearances were momentary but meaningful. They confirmed faith in God, and urged the believers to continue spreading the good news of eternal life made possible through the grace of God in Jesus Messiah.

Paul's testimony to resurrection-life is the most poignant in the New Testament, especially in 1 Cor 15. I suspect the Corinthian gentiles questioned the very idea of resurrection from among the dead. The Sadducees of Judaism were equally as skeptical of the possibility of resurrection. The Pharisees not so much. Paul was a Pharisee who surrendered his life to the call of Jesus Messiah resurrected. Let me simply quote the essence of his argument for resurrection life, this coming from one who witnessed an appearance of the resurrected Jesus, and one who knows how to frame a compelling argument.

> Now if Christ is proclaimed as raised from the dead, how can some of you say there is no resurrection of the dead? If there is no resurrection of the dead, then Christ has not been raised; and if Christ has not been raised, then our proclamation has been in vain and your faith has been in vain. We are even found to be misrepresenting God, because we testified of God that he raised Christ—whom he did not raise if it is true that the dead are not raised. (1 Cor 15:12–15)

You see what I mean about Paul's ability to make a case as a lawyer might. One more citation from 1 Corinthians must suffice.

> So it is with the resurrection of the dead. What is sown is perishable, what is raised is imperishable. It is sown in dishonor, it is raised in glory. It is sown in weakness, it is raised in power. It is sown a physical body, it is raised a spiritual body. If there is a physical body, there is also a spiritual body. Thus it is written, "The first man, Adam, became a living being"; the last Adam became a life-giving spirit. But it is not the spiritual that is first, but the physical, and then the spiritual. (1 Cor 15:42–46)

If Paul were here in this moment I might be inclined to ask him this: "Is a spiritual body real?" I'm not sure how he would answer. He might respond with a rhetorical question such as this: "Is the invisible air we breath to sustain life real?"

Moreover, a case for a physical, bodily resurrection, exactly equal to the physical body of Jesus prior to his death, is untenable. That something significant happened to the disciples shortly after the crucifixion of Jesus should be reckoned as "real." Despite the suffering inflicted on their Leader, which could quickly fall on them, they forged ahead in mission in the name Jesus as the promised Messiah of God whose Spirit filled their hearts and minds for the trials they were bound to encounter from the vested powers of the time.

16

Conclusion

The Disposition of Love in the Context of the Fourth Gospel

I DON'T WANT THIS concluding chapter to be a mere summary of the content in the foregoing chapters. I doubt such an approach would prove helpful. Instead, I prefer to highlight some significant features within and around the Fourth Gospel that have helped me understand its many-sided story. I shall postpone the specific topic of "the disposition of love" until the end.

It is my hope that these few pointers will spur the reader on to gain more and more insight into the contours and contexts that make this unique Gospel of the New Testament so captivating to so many people of faith. Admittedly, not everyone is drawn to this Gospel equally. Some people find it far-reaching and mysterious, compared to the Synoptic Gospels. I understand their reaction. At the same time, the Fourth Gospel was incorporated into the canon of the New Testament, and by that token alone it calls for our unreserved effort to grapple with its portrait of Jesus in his time and place and situation, which helped pave the way forward for early Christianity at the dawn of the second century.

A Complicated Love Story

SITUATION IN THE LIFE OF THE COMMUNITY
OUT OF WHICH THIS GOSPEL COMES

It may seem strange to signal the situation surrounding the new Christian movement at the beginning of the second century of the Common Era. After all, the obvious content-and-context of the Fourth Gospel appears to be about Jesus, Galilee, his disciples, Judaism, Jerusalem, and the temple at about 30 CE. That is true. But the author was not a local Jewish reporter on location in Palestine writing about the events as they were taking place. On the contrary, the situation in the life of the author and his community happened more likely at the end of the first century, or the beginning of the second. That later community was the target audience for this unique Gospel aimed at strengthening the verve and the faith of that later beloved group of believers in Jesus as Messiah. It could hardly be otherwise.

Accordingly, the modern interpreter would do well to keep that feature in mind to make sense of some of the puzzling parts of the narrative. For example, what are we to make of an implicitly powerful group in the Fourth Gospel broadly identified as "the Jews"? Does that include the whole spectrum of Jewish people everywhere in the Roman world? Or is one specific group of Jewish *leaders* implicitly in focus? Or are there several alternatives? Notably absent from the narrative are the Sadducees. That group of Jews was squelched during the Roman conquest of Jerusalem. They were a rather significant group in Palestine at the time of Jesus. Pharisees *are* identified in the Fourth Gospel, and also their knowledgeable teachers of the Law, called rabbis (1:38; 3:2). That group survived the bloody war of 66–70 CE. More on that point later.

Chief among the varied experiences in the Christian community at the time of writing was the tug-of-war between reconstituted Judaism apart from faith in Jesus Messiah, on the one hand, and the new community of faith in Jesus Messiah, on the other. That tension should not be taken lightly in the interpretation of the Fourth Gospel. Among the Jewish converts to Christianity were some who doubtless wished they could belong to both communities of faith. They were still Jews, as Jesus was. Both the rabbis and the Christians were using the same Scriptures, and worshiping the same God. The difference came down to one tenet of faith: the Christians believed that Messiah had come, while "the Jews" did not so believe. The result was that some Jewish-born members in the Christian community were barred from the rabbinic Jewish community. Little by little, Jewish adherents of the community of Christians had to make a choice between Rabbinic Judaism on the one hand, and the new community of faith in Jesus Messiah on the other. The stated purpose in writing the Fourth Gospel implies as much: "Now Jesus did many other signs in the presence of his disciples, which are not written in this book. *But these are written so that you may come to believe that Jesus is the Messiah, the son of God, and that through believing you may have life in his name*" (20:30).

Let me explain in more detail the life situation in the community of faith in Jesus Messiah at the time of writing the Fourth Gospel. Much had happened since the earlier time in the life of Jesus and his disciples in Palestine. The new situation in the life of the community of the Beloved Disciple at the onset of the second century was bound to affect the way the author told the long story about Jesus, his disciples, his public ministry, and his death and resurrection, all of which happened about sixty to seventy years earlier. Principal among the intervening events, carried out by the Roman militia in 66–70 CE, was the ruthless destruction of the Holy City of Jerusalem, together with its magnificent temple on Mount Zion, and not least the cruel death of many Jewish citizens of Jerusalem. Well-known Jewish sects were eradicated as a result: Sadducees, Essenes, and Zealots. The only Jewish group that survived the horror of the Roman War against the Judean Jews was the Pharisees. Most of the outlying Jewish peasant farmers of Palestine also escaped the onslaught. But the religion of Judaism could scarcely sustain its distinctive identity for long by relying on the good will and hard work of nonliterate "people of the land." That task fell to an educated Jewish group, the rabbis.

Rome granted permission to the Pharisees, later called rabbis, to set up a headquarters in the town of Jamnia in Gaza, well away from the site of Jerusalem. Why would the Jewish "Pharisees" drop that title? The name means, "separated ones." In their new headquarters the "separated ones" were no longer separated from other Jewish groups, because other Jewish groups had disappeared after 70 CE. There was the religion of Judaism still in the Diaspora, and there were the "people of the land" in Palestine. But who would be responsible for keeping the Jewish people faithful to their identity as Jews, and to their Scriptures and their traditions? The rabbis filled that role as teachers of Jewish law, worship, and service. But the Pharisees of the temple period were not the only ones to reconstitute themselves after the Jewish war in Palestine. There was the new community of Jesus the Jew, acknowledged by his followers as Messiah and Savior. This brings us to the point about understanding the contours and context of the Fourth Gospel from the vantage point of later development.

THE NEW JEW-AND-GENTILE COMMUNITY OF JESUS MESSIAH UNDER PRESSURE

The community of Jesus Messiah also survived the onslaught, even though the Roman overlords executed some of the principal leaders shortly before the outbreak of the Jewish War in Palestine in 66 CE. Apostles Peter and Paul were among the martyrs. Yet groups of believers in Jesus Messiah continued undeterred across Asia Minor and elsewhere. They could be found active in principal cities such as Rome, Corinth, Philippi, and Antioch, among others. These groups maintained a communal witness to Jesus Messiah, even after the untimely death of noteworthy apostles. They identified their groups as "called-out people," *ekklêsiai*, usually rendered "churches."

James, the brother of Jesus, also suffered painful death by stoning in 62 CE at the hands of a rogue high priest (Hanan ben Hanan). Despite these tragic deaths of Jewish Christian leaders, communities of believers prevailed, including the community reflected in the Fourth Gospel. In its earliest development, following the death of Jesus, the Christ-followers in Jerusalem were Jews. The communities that formed outside Palestine, as a result of the mission of Paul and others, were made up of both Jews and gentiles. As the second century unfolded, fewer and fewer hereditary Jews remained in the Christian communities. By the middle of the second century the Christian churches were made up largely of gentiles. The Fourth Gospel seems to be aimed—in part at least—at encouraging both Jewish and gentile Christ-followers to remain faithful to the new community of Jesus Messiah, with its roots in traditional Judaism.

The precise location of that distinctive Christian community, or church (*ekklêsia*), represented in the Fourth Gospel is a matter of debate. Some locale in Asia Minor is a fairly safe guess. Asia Minor is a large area. More specifically, the Christian community implicit in the Fourth Gospel may have settled in Antioch of Syria, a key city in the development of Christian mission to the gentile world. These place-names are guesses at best. That there was such a distinctive community of Jewish and gentile Christians is confirmed by four documents of the New Testament that bear similar literary, theological, and communal characteristics. One is the Fourth Gospel, of course, and the other three are short letters under the title name "John"

(For more on the distinctive character of this Christian community, I recommend the insightful book by Raymond E. Brown, *The Community of the Beloved Disciple: The Life, Loves and Hates of an Individual Church in New Testament Times*).

THE UNIQUENESS OF THE FOURTH GOSPEL ALONGSIDE THE THREE SYNOPTIC GOSPELS

It would be well to address the difference between the group of three Synoptic Gospels and the Fourth Gospel. The Fourth Gospel is clearly *not* aligned with any of the three Synoptic Gospels. The question is this: Would the author of the Fourth Gospel have knowledge of any or all of the Synoptic Gospels, and chose not to use any part of them? It appears to be the case. As we discovered, he echoes parts of the Synoptic Gospels with which he disagreed. Thereby he chose not to align his Gospel with any of the Synoptic writings, or the Synoptic tradition they represent. We know this by virtue of the correction the Fourth Evangelist made to some key points. Three stand out, related as they are to the suffering death of Jesus.

One of the most obvious is the time when Jesus entered the court of the temple to chase out the animals and overturn the tables of the moneychangers. The Synoptic Evangelists put that event in the last week of the ministry of Jesus, whereas the Fourth Gospel puts it at the beginning of the ministry of Jesus. Some scholars argue that the action of Jesus clearing the temple court precipitated his trial that led to his crucifixion by the end of the same week. According to the timeline in the Fourth Gospel, however, the ministry of Jesus lasted about three years after the clearing of the temple court.

While the Synoptic writers cite Simon of Cyrene as the one to carry the cross of Jesus to the place of crucifixion, the Fourth Evangelist makes the point sharply that Jesus went forth "carrying the cross *by himself*" (19:17). Similarly, the Synoptic Gospels have Jesus in the garden of Gethsemane praying to God thus: "remove this cup [of suffering] from me" (Mark 14:36). In the Fourth Gospel Jesus prays otherwise about the same situation: "Now my soul is troubled. And what should I say—'Father, save me from this hour'? *No*, it is for this reason that I have come to this hour" (12:27). Similarly, "Jesus said to Peter, 'Am I not to drink the cup that the Father has given me?'" (18:11).

Assuming, thus, that the Fourth Evangelist was aware of the Synoptic Gospels, especially Matthew and Luke, his Prologue (1:1–18) effectively sets aside the high honor ascribed to Mary by Matthew and especially by Luke. The theological Prologue about Jesus's entrance into the physical world proffers not even a scintilla of credit to the virgin, Mary. The full and unequivocal credit goes to God in relationship with the *logos*-son: "And the Word became flesh and lived among us, and we have seen his glory, the glory as of a father's only son, full of grace and truth" (1:14). Rather than giving credit to Mary of Nazareth for bearing Jesus in her womb and delivering him to the world, the Fourth Evangelist points to the witness of John the Baptist: "John testified to [Jesus] and cried out, 'This was he of whom I said, "He who comes after me ranks ahead of me because he was before me."'" (1:15). The role of Mary in bringing Jesus into human history is essentially rendered inoperative by the Fourth Evangelist.

If my hunch is correct, that the author of the Fourth Gospel was aware of the Synoptic Gospels, then the Prologue that highlights Jesus's entrance into the human family implicitly discounts the birth narratives of Luke and Matthew. The coming of Jesus as Son of God to the world needed not the blessed virgin to make it happen. Had the Fourth Evangelist been alive when the later bishops of the church created the creeds, one can imagine what his reaction might have been to the later liturgical language of worship that hailed Mary of Nazareth as the virgin "Mother of God."

THE EFFECT OF ANONYMITY WHERE ONE MIGHT NOT EXPECT IT

Continuing for a moment on the role of the mother of Jesus in the Fourth Gospel, we find her to be completely anonymous. Not once does the narrator give her proper name, "Mary." Twice Jesus addresses his mother directly, not as "mother" or as "Mary," but as "woman." The first is in the context of the wedding at Cana of Galilee when his hour had not yet come, and the second at the scene of crucifixion when his hour had come. In both instances Jesus addresses his mother directly as "woman," where one might expect "mother." He also addresses the woman of Samaria as "woman." In that instance, however, one would expect as much. The Samaritan woman was not well-known to him, and she was certainly not his mother. His mother, by contrast, had nurtured him through infancy and

CONCLUSION

adolescence. Yet the form of address in both settings appears to distance Jesus from his mother. Let me repeat, I suspect that the scrolls of the Gospels of Matthew and Luke were in circulation, and known to the Fourth Evangelist. He implicitly diminishes the high and holy honor bestowed on Mary by those two Synoptic Evangelists in their introductory chapters.

In keeping with the anonymity of the mother of Jesus, his brothers likewise are not named. We know their names from Mark and Matthew: "James and Joses and Judas and Simon" (Mark 6:3). It seems that given names proffer not only identify, but also status. The sole figure in the Fourth Gospel who deserves both identity and status is Jesus Messiah from beginning to end. His identity comes not merely from his filial relationship with his mother or brothers, but from his unique relationship to Father-God. The Prologue makes that abundantly obvious. That Jesus was born of Mary of Nazareth is doubtless true historically. But the Fourth Evangelist will not allow that factor to interfere with the principal factor of the divine origin of Jesus. So the brothers of Jesus are with him, but not named. Brother James in particular became the principal leader of the Christian community in Jerusalem following the death of his brother Jesus at about 30 CE. James continued in that leadership role until his untimely death in 62 CE. I have no doubt that the author of the Fourth Gospel knew that fact very well, but chose not to identify James by name or by his relationship to Jesus.

The most striking instance of anonymity in the Fourth Gospel comes in the book of the Passion. I refer, of course, to the nameless disciple known only by the title "the disciple whom Jesus loved" (13:23; 20:2; 21:7, 20). It is ever so tempting to replace the literary motif of anonymity with a proper name. But the act of doing so robs the narrative of its deliberate use of *characterization* in the absence of a proper name. I have found through the years that readers of the Fourth Gospel feel more at home with supplying a proper name for the anonymous characters in the narrative. I am among them. But I do try hard to curb my urge, so as to allow the narrator of the Fourth Gospel to perform his literary work without my interference.

The effect of giving one disciple a designation rather than a proper given name tends to draw the reader into the story. Moreover, the anonymity of the disciple whom Jesus loved has the effect of prompting the reader to ask: "How could I become such a beloved disciple?" "What characteristics did that disciple have to prompt Jesus to love him above all others?" I tend to want to know the given names of people that I encounter. (Recall that I could not resist putting forward the name of James the brother of Jesus as the most likely candidate to fill the role of "beloved disciple.") But lately I have found myself drawn to "character" rather than a proper name. Put otherwise, I would prefer that people know me first and foremost by the content of my character, and secondarily by my given name.

THE THEMATIC DISPOSITION OF LOVE

There are two Greek words in the Fourth Gospel translated with one English word "love": *philos* and *agapê*. These two Greek nouns also appear as verbs. It would seem, then, that we have no English word to distinguish the sense of one word for love from the other. *Philos* appears in the first part of the English word "philosophy." The second part of the word is "sophia," wisdom. Hence the basic sense of the word "philosophy" is "love of wisdom." But in the Fourth Gospel the other Greek noun and verb for love, *agapê/agapaō*, dominates. Compared to *philos/phileo*, which occurs thirteen times in the Fourth Gospel, the word *agapê/agapaō* appears thirty-seven times.

There is a story behind the meaning of *agapê/agapaō* in the Greek version of the Hebrew Bible that appeared around 200 BCE. I hereby credit C. H. Dodd for the measure of insight he provided on this matter.[12]

When the Jewish scribes of Alexandria in Egypt found it necessary to translate the Hebrew Bible into Greek for the Jews of Diaspora, many of whom were not very familiar with Hebrew, some Hebrew terms did not translate well into Greek. One Hebrew word in particular presented a problem (*chesed*). It is translated into English with two words in the NRSV: "steadfast love." It signals the unwavering love of God for the people of Israel. When the Greek translators came to this deeply significant Hebrew word they sought for a distinctive equivalent in Greek, but came up empty at first. Then the translators came upon the word *agape/agapaō* in Greek that was not widely used either in literature or in everyday speech. The Jewish scribes of Alexandria latched onto this little-used Greek word and loaded it up with meaning to represent the invariable love and grace of God that never fails. That Greek word for "love" (*agape/agapaō*) thereby came into the Greek New Testament, particularly the Fourth Gospel, to represent the unfailing love of God in the person of Jesus, Son of God. Its abundance

---

12. Dodd, *Interpretation of the Fourth Gospel*, 398–99. See also Lewis, *Four Loves*, 141–70.

in the Fourth Gospel becomes thematic. I should point out, however, that the more common verb for love, *phileō*, occurs only once to identify the "disciple whom Jesus loved" (20:2). A distinction between the two terms translated "love" should still be maintained. Otherwise, the three-part structure of the test of Peter's love for Jesus, recorded in the Appendix at 21:15–17, would be meaningless.

I would be remiss, in closing, if I did not draw attention to the role of the loving, life-giving Spirit of God in the Fourth Gospel. Without the operation of the Spirit of God there could be no hope of eternal life, for "God is spirit, and those who worship [God] must worship in spirit and truth" (4:24). In the same vein, the metaphor of spiritual birth appears prominently in chapter 3. The implication of the birth metaphor is that human thoughts, words, and actions, however well-intentioned and executed, cannot attain eternal life. Furthermore, natural birth does not happen by intention and activity of the baby, but by the sensation and action of the mother. That is the metaphysics implicit in the metaphor.

In short, birth from above is initiated and executed by the will and power of God. When a well-meaning evangelical person asks someone—as happened to me—if they are "born again" the questioner usually means: "Was there a time and place and circumstance when you asked Jesus to come into your heart?" That thought pattern stands in stark contrast to the imagery in 3:3–9, "born from above" (*gennêthênai anōthen*). The Spirit that brings about that kind of birth is compared to the behavior of the wind that blows where and when it will. No human ingenuity can catch and hold the wind. There is no mantra that will make the wind physically visible and manageable. "The wind blows where it chooses, and you hear the sound of it, but you do not know where it comes from or where it goes. So it is with everyone who is born of the Spirit" (3:8). Moreover, any human intentionality that takes full credit for birth from above by mere human decision-making, could end up implicitly thinking along the line of the modern song, "I did it my way." The wording of the text of 3:3–9 should come across to our mind as it stands in the text. Pressing it into a mold generated by human inclination, or ill-informed theological imagination, violates its focus. The new kind of birth "from above" comes ultimately from the Spirit of God.

Bibliography

Anderson, Paul N. *The Riddles of the Fourth Gospel: An Introduction to John*. Minneapolis: Fortress, 2011.
Ashton, John, ed. *The Interpretation of John*. Issues in Religion and Theology 9. Philadelphia: Fortress, 1986.
Barrett, C. K. *The Gospel of John and Judaism*. Translated from the German by D. M. Smith. Philadelphia: Fortress, 1975.
Barth, Karl. *Witness to the Word: A Commentary on John 1*. Edited by Walter Furst and translated by Geoffrey W. Bromiley. Eugene, OR: Wipf & Stock, 2003.
Bauckham, Richard, and Carl Mosser, eds. *The Gospel of John and Christian Theology*. Grand Rapids: Eerdmans, 2008.
Bell, Lonnie D. *The Early Textual Transmission of John: Stability and Fluidity in its Second and Third Century Greek Manuscripts*. Leiden: Brill, 2018.
Brown, Raphael. *The Life of Mary As Seen by the Mystics*. Repr. Kettering: Angelico, 2014.
Brown, Raymond E. *The Community of the Beloved Disciple*. New York: Paulist, 1979.
Brown, Raymond E., with Francis J. Moloney. *An Introduction to the Gospel of John*. 1st ed. Anchor Yale Bible Reference Library. New Haven, CT: Yale University, 2003.
Bultmann, Rudolf. *The Gospel of John: A Commentary*. The Johannine Monograph Series. Foreword by Paul N. Anderson. Eugene, OR: Wipf & Stock, 2014.
Carroll, Donald. *Mary's House: The Extraordinary Story Behind the Discovery of the House Where the Virgin Mary Lived and Died*. London: Veritas, 2000.
Crossan, John Dominic. *How to Read the Bible and Still be a Christian: Struggling with Divine Violence from Genesis through Revelation*. New York: HarperOne, 2015.
Culpepper, R. Alan. *Anatomy of the Fourth Gospel: A Study in Literary Design*. Foundations and Facets: New Testament. Philadelphia: Fortress, 1987.
Diel, Paul, and Jeannine Solotareff. *Symbolism in the Gospel of John*. Translated by Nelly Marans. San Francisco: Harper & Row, 1988.
Dickens, Charles. *A Tale of Two Cities*. N.p.: CreateSpace, 2015.
Dodd, C. H. *The Interpretation of the Fourth Gospel*. Cambridge: Cambridge University Press, 1953.
Duke, Paul D. *Irony in the Fourth Gospel*. Atlanta: John Knox, 1985.
Filson, Floyd V. *The Gospel of John*. The Layman's Bible Commentary 19. Richmond: John Knox, 1972.
Fredriksen, Paula. *Jesus of Nazareth, King of the Jews: A Jewish Life and the Emergence of Christianity*. New York: Vintage, 2000.
Harpur, Tom. *Would You Believe? Finding God Without Losing Your Mind*. Toronto: McClelland & Stewart, 1996.
Hawking, Stephen. *A Brief History of Time: The Updated and Expanded Tenth Anniversary Edition*. New York: Bantam, 1996.

Bibliography

Howell, Elizabeth. "How Many Galaxies Are There?" https://www.space.com/25303-how-many-galaxies-are-in-the-universe.html.

Hunt, Steven A., et al., eds. *Character Studies in the Fourth Gospel: Narrative Approaches to Seventy Figures in John*. Grand Rapids: Eerdmans, 2016.

Jervell, Jacob. *Jesus in the Gospel of John*. Translated by Harry T. Cleven. Minneapolis: Augsburg, 1984.

Keener, Craig S. *The Gospel of John: A Commentary*. 2 vols. Peabody, MA: Hendrickson, 2003.

Lewis, C. S. *The Four Loves*. London: Bles, 1960.

Martyn, J. Louis. *History and Theology in the Fourth Gospel*. New Testament Library. 3rd ed. Louisville: Westminster John Knox, 2003.

Meyer, Ben F. *Critical Realism and the New Testament*. Allison Park, PA: Pickwick, 1989.

Michaels, J. Ramsey. *The Gospel of John*. New International Commentary on the New Testament. Grand Rapids: Eerdmans, 2010.

Morris, Leon. *Reflections on the Gospel of John*. Vol. 1, *The Word Was Made Flesh*. Grand Rapids: Baker, 1986.

Muggeridge, Malcolm. *Jesus Rediscovered*. Garden City, NY: Doubleday, 1969.

Nederhood, Joel H. *The Forever People: Living Today in the Light of Eternity*. Grand Rapids: CRC Publications, 2000.

Neyrey, Jerome H. *The Gospel of John*. New Cambridge Bible Commentary. New York: Cambridge University Press, 2007.

Reinhartz, Adele. *Befriending the Beloved Disciple: A Jewish Reading of the Gospel of John*. New York: Continuum, 2001.

Rensberger, David. *Johannine Faith and Liberating Community*. Louisville: Westminster John Knox, 1996.

Rivkin, Ellis. *What Crucified Jesus?: Messianism, Pharisaism, and the Development of Christianity*. New York: Union for Reform Judaism, 1997.

Sanders, E. P. *The Historical Figure of Jesus*. London: Penguin, 1996.

Shillington, V. George. *James and Paul: The Politics of Identity at the Turn of the Ages*. Minneapolis: Fortress, 2015.

———. *Jesus and Paul Before Christianity*. Eugene, OR: Cascade, 2011.

———. "The Legendary James the Just." In *James and Paul: the Politics of Identity at the Turn of the Ages*, 121–50. Minneapolis: Fortress, 2015.

———. *Reading the Sacred Text: An Introduction in Biblical Studies*. London: T. & T. Clark, 2002.

———. "Significant Translation: Exchange as Literary-Theological Pattern in John." *Direction* 33.2 (2004) 158–70.

Spong, John Shelby. *The Fourth Gospel: Tales of a Jewish Mystic*. New York: HarperCollins, 2014.

Theodore, Bishop of Mopsuestia. *Commentary on the Gospel of John*. Translated with an introduction and notes by Marco Conti. Edited by Joel C. Elowsky. Ancient Christian Texts. Downers Grove, IL: IVP Academic, 2010.

Thompson, Marianne Meye. *The God of the Gospel of John*. Grand Rapids: Eerdmans, 2001.

Vermes, Geza. *Jesus the Jew: A Historian's Reading of the Gospels*. Minneapolis: Fortress, 1981.

CPSIA information can be obtained
at www.ICGtesting.com
Printed in the USA
LVHW042029031119
636213LV00001B/39/P